The LONG- DISTANCE DAD

How You Can Be There for Your Child—Whether Divorced, Deployed, or on the Road

STEVEN ASHLEY, Founder, Divorced Fathers Network
with Philip S. Hall, Ph.D.

Aadamsmedia
avon, massachusetts

Published by
Adams Media, an F+W Publications Company
57 Littlefield Street, Avon, MA 02322. U.S.A.
www.adamsmedia.com

ISBN 10: 1-59869-441-3
ISBN 13: 978-1-59869-441-3

Printed in the United States of America.

J I H G F E D C B A

Library of Congress Cataloging-in-Publication Data
is available from the publisher.

This publication is designed to provide accurate and authoritative
information with regard to the subject matter covered. It is sold with
the understanding that the publisher is not engaged in rendering
legal, accounting, or other professional advice. If legal advice or other
expert assistance is required, the services of a competent professional
person should be sought.
—From a *Declaration of Principles* jointly adopted by a
Committee of the American Bar Association and
a Committee of Publishers and Associations

Many of the designations used by manufacturers and sellers to distin-
guish their product are claimed as trademarks. Where those designations appear in this book and Adams Media was aware of a trademark
claim, the designations have been printed with initial capital letters.

This book is available at quantity discounts for bulk purchases.
For information, please call 1-800-289-0963.

Dedicated to the thousands of long-distance dads
I spoke with during the past twenty years.

Your commitment to your children is inspiring.

Acknowledgments

First and foremost, I am indebted to my wife, Susan—her support of my efforts to assist fathers has never wavered. She has listened to my ideas, offered suggestions, and assisted me in completing my goals. I will be forever grateful.

The volunteers in the Divorced Fathers Network have my respect and appreciation. Their willingness to teach co-parenting skills, free of charge, to both fathers and mothers enables more parents to be involved in their children's lives; in turn, families and communities are happier and healthier.

Many thanks to Paula Munier, her understanding of the importance of fathers to children and family made this book possible. If every person understood, with her passion, how important fathers are to children, there would be more resources available to fathers.

Finally, thanks to all my friends and family who listen to my stories of Long-Distance Dads and their struggles. It is almost assured that wherever I go, there will be discussion of fathers and the need for them. Not one of my friends or family members has ever said, "Enough already." Maybe that affirms the fact that fathers are important.

Contents

1

Becoming a Long-Distance Dad

SO YOU'RE A "LONG-DISTANCE DAD." WHAT IS a long-distance dad? Who is a long-distance dad? Put simply, long-distance dads are men who find themselves in one place and their children in another. This book is for fathers determined to raise emotionally resilient, psychologically stable, confident, and independent children.

The Many Faces of Long-Distance Parenting

You're already a good father. Now you can be a great father no matter where you are because you bought this book. Note that the phrase is "long-distance parenting," not "long-distance fathering." Think about the difference between the words "father" and "mother." Now think of these words as verbs, rather than as nouns. Language is a culture carrier, and as such, it reflects our biases, our perceptions of the world around us, many of them ingrained and unconscious.

In English, "fathering" a child means little more than having sex with the mother so that she, in turn, conceives a child. Now think about the difference between the verb form of "father" and the verb form of "mother." According to *Webster's Dictionary*, the word "father," when used as a verb, means "to beget." On the other hand, the word "mother" is defined as "to care for, or protect like a mother."

So, according to the unconscious shorthand of the English language, fathers have sex for procreation, and mothers raise children. Add to this the relatively twentieth-century notion that fathers are breadwinners, and mothers are nurturers, and you've got a recipe for the irrelevancy of the modern male in child rearing.

How ironic that the last decade or so of the twentieth century gave rise to the notion that women, who had been entering the workforce in larger and larger numbers during the previous half century, had now begun an exodus back out of the ranks of the employed once they'd had a child. As recently as July 2007, articles with titles such as "Full-Time Work Losing Luster for Moms" appeared in newspapers like the *Washington Post*. Imagine the hue and cry if you substituted the word "Dads" for "Moms." If you are one of those who winced at the notion of cutting back on your workday in order to help parent your children, then this book is written with you in mind. This is true whether you're divorced, whether you're married with kids and on the road all the time, whether you're incarcerated, or whether you're in the military and deployed away from your children.

The reason why this book is for you is because it will help you re-educate that portion of your brain that hangs almost all of your self-worth on the notion of successful breadwinning. For example, it may have never occurred to you to take some time off from work in order to help raise your kids, but try looking at it another way: imagine that less time spent earning a living is the price of building a stronger bond with your kids. What father in his right mind would want to forego that?!

This sort of trade-off is not as uncommon as you might otherwise think. The days of the old stereotype of fathers not being as important a part of the parenting process are over. Long-distance fathers come in all shapes and sizes, from all walks of life, and from every age. Examples of this type of long-distance dad include business travelers, twenty-first century "road warriors," men either climbing or already atop the corporate ladder; divorced, noncustodial parents; fathers in the armed forces; traveling salespeople; bus drivers; truckers; professional athletes; musicians and entertainers. This broad umbrella also includes physically or psychologically challenged parents; disabled parents; grandparents; incarcerated dads; and any other guys who have to be away from their children for a week, a month, or in some cases, for even longer.

If you're a divorced parent (and with the current rate of divorce in this country currently sitting at over two million per year, there are more and more of you every day), you know that the trend is toward divorce and physical relocation of children (away from one of their parents), not away from the idea of parents and children staying together. And with issues such as child support and the need to continue to parent with your former spouse even after the divorce becomes final, you need all the help you can get. After all, just because you're divorced from your ex doesn't mean that you want to have an ex-kid.

If you're one of the "road warriors," you'll see how business travelers stack up as fathers when compared to the more traditional nine-to-five dad. In this day and age, with men looking for work, moving from one part of the country to another (or even from one country/continent to another), checking out opportunity after opportunity, their children are facing adversity right there with them (even if they're not in close physical proximity). In many cases, children don't know where Dad is likely to turn up and how long he is likely to be away.

Maybe you're one of these "long-distance granddads." If you are, then you're no doubt "fathering" your own adult children, and in turn you're sometimes acting as a surrogate parent (frequently a long-distance one) who provides both emotional and financial support not just for his children, but for grandchildren who may lack an immediate male role model in their lives for any of a variety of reasons (such as their own father being absent).

One particularly common variety of long-distance dad is the military dad. Especially these days, with so many members of the military reserves and national guard units being called up (sometimes repeatedly) for active duty overseas, the military long-distance dad is more prevalent today than at any time since the end of World War II. This statistic might sound odd to you, but it is true because the majority of those going overseas to Vietnam were single men with no children. Just because you're posted overseas or across the country and temporarily away from your family doesn't mean that you stop being responsible or stop caring for your children. In fact, your spouse will no doubt value every little bit of help that you as their father can give, regardless of the physical distance the separates you.

Some Statistics for Long-Distance Dads

Nothing does more to ensure a child's overall well-being than the presence of a father figure in his or her life. For example, in publishing a recent survey on child health, the U.S. Department of Health and Human Services reported, "Fatherless children are at dramatically greater risk for drug and alcohol abuse, mental illness, suicide, poor educational performance, teen pregnancy, and criminality." Furthermore, the *National Principals Association Report on the State of High Schools* reports that "71% of all high school dropouts come from fatherless homes."

And how much does the presence of a father in a child's life contribute to their peace of mind? The U.S. Census Bureau found that "63% of youth suicides are from fatherless homes." The Centers for Disease Control reports that "85% of all children that exhibit behavioral disorders come from fatherless homes."

Your children need your involvement in their lives for more than just financial and emotional support, though. As a father, you also are highly likely to impact your child's actual physical safety as well. Clearly fathers shield their children from crime and make communities safer places to live. A 1988 special report from the U.S. Department of Justice found that 70 percent of underaged offenders in state-operated institutions came from homes where there was no father figure. Perhaps the most shocking statistic you'll see about children raised without a father in their lives is this one from the Centers for Disease Control: "80% of rapists motivated with displaced anger come from fatherless homes."

Put in layman's terms, a child from a fatherless home is:

- 5 times more likely to commit suicide
- 9 times more likely to drop out of school
- 9 times more likely to end up in a state-operated institution
- 10 times more likely to abuse chemical substances
- 14 times more likely to commit rape

- 20 times more likely to have behavioral disorders
- 20 times more likely to end up in prison
- 32 times more likely to run away from home

So, there you have it. If your children are emotionally bonded with you, they are more apt to have high self-esteem and to avoid drug use, alcoholism, incarceration, and teen pregnancy.

Kids who regularly see their dads are more likely to graduate from high school, to attend college, and to enjoy a successful marriage. What's more, children with involved fathers do better in school, exhibit higher levels of emotional well-being, and have an easier time making friends, *even if* their father does not live with them. You as a father are vital to the emotional, financial, and physical health of your children.

Successful adults tend to praise their fathers' parenting skills. For example, many successful businesswomen often credit their fathers with instilling in them the belief that they could succeed in corporate America, that the glass ceiling is no match for them, that their place is in the boardroom, and so on. And almost any adult male can tell you about the number of times that fatherly advice saved him from grief later on (assuming that he took it!).

But what about you? It turns out that good emotional and physical health are two-way streets when it comes to American families. Fathers who are active participants in family life report lower levels of both stress and depression, coupled with higher levels of satisfaction with their overall quality of life. There are other rewards of parenting as well, such as the importance of guiding a young person's life, the joy of staying youthful yourself by becoming caught up in a young person's activities, and finding that involvement in a child's world expands your own world and friendships.

In this book, you'll find suggestions, tips, examples, success stories, and a variety of schema intended to help you successfully navigate the rocks and shoals of being actively involved in your child's life no matter what your physical distance from your child. Let's take a moment to touch briefly on a few of these right now. We will explore each of these concepts in more depth in future chapters.

Keep the Lines of Communication Open

Although there's never going to be an ideal time to be a long-distance dad, if you're going to have to be one, now is the best time so far. With the advances our society has made in communication technology over the past couple of decades, you are not restricted to either the postal system or an expensive long-distance calling plan in order to be able to maintain contact with your child.

Thanks to things like webcams, you don't even need to wait until your children are old enough to read and write in order to be able to interact effectively with them. On top of that you also have things like cellular phone calling plans that will allow your children to get a hold of you (and vice versa) anytime that they need or want to. Having unfettered, unrestricted access to your child, regardless of the physical distance currently between you, is one of the cornerstones of building a successful relationship with your child, and is a key tool in your ongoing struggle not to retreat into the fog and become a virtual stranger to them.

Of course, with those children who are old enough to read and write, you've got a couple of other valuable technological tools available to you in your quest to keep in close contact with them: e-mail accounts and chat programs. Both help cut the distance out of the miles between you. We'll revisit these and other electronic means of staying close to your children in a later chapter.

Strengthening the Bond Between You and Your Kids

Sometimes the toughest thing for you as a father is to understand your child. Note that by "understand" I am not implying "agree with." This is particularly true with regard to discipline. If you can discipline your children with care and understanding, you can do anything. Why? Simple. Discipline administered with understanding shows your kids that you're not some drill master insisting on blind regard for an arbitrary set of rules made up by you and obeyed by them. Discipline administered in this manner displays caring, and a kid who knows that you care about him or her while also providing a healthily structured environment is already ten times less likely to drop out of school than a child reared in a more "chaotic" environment is.

"But wait," you say. "This section is not titled 'Disciplining Your Child,' it's titled, 'Strengthening the Bond Between You and Your Kids.' So why this talk about discipline?"

Once again, the answer is simple, and you'll read this phrase over and over again in the course of reading this book: *kids crave structure*. Bonds between human beings are strengthened by such things as shared experiences, working as a team, showing commitment (remember that word, more on it below) to each other, and demonstrated compassion. Even a rebellious teenager craves the sort of structure that successful parenting provides in the home, if for no other reason than that it gives the kid something against which to rebel, and something to come back to once that rebellion is (hopefully) out of the kid's system.

However, as I mentioned above, structure is only half of the equation. Structure in its own right is nothing more than a framework, a skeleton on which to hang the skin, heart, and kidneys of compassion, the neural network of understanding. Do you think it's possible to love your kids without understanding them? Sure thing. Is it possible to love them without compassion for them? As objects, certainly. But if you love them, you've got to know them, and knowing them means understanding them. It's not enough to simply understand them, though; you've got to demonstrate it. And that can be a tough row to hoe for some of us big, bad, manly types. More on this in Chapter 2.

Maintain Good Ties with the Mother of Your Children

Maybe you've picked up this book because you're separated from your children's mother. Maybe you're already divorced. Maybe you're married (happily or otherwise) and either on the road a lot or deployed overseas.

Whatever the legal status of your relationship with the mother of your children, the fact is that you have one, and you're going to have one for the rest of your life, regardless of the age of your kids. If you hadn't thought of that before, here's your reality check: you have a relationship that ought to be prioritized, if not as highly as, nearly as highly as your relationship with your kids.

Setting aside notions of right and wrong (in the case of divorced long-distance dads) and fair distribution of parenting resources (in the case of road-warrior and deployed dads), the pragmatic side of your brain (and men are the "logical" ones, or at least seem to be the gender that most takes pride in being so) ought to tell you that maintaining the best possible relationship with the mother of your children is *in your best interest*! This is someone who can be either an ally in the struggle to raise healthy, emotionally independent adults or a thorn in your side, the one who is always turning your kids against you, bad-mouthing you to them, et cetera.

The long and the short of it is that the relationship between you and the mother of your children, like all relationships, takes effort, and making it a priority is just one more thing on what likely constitutes a massive daily to-do list on your part. But if you're in your logical male mode, stop for a moment and conduct what our economist friends call a "cost-benefit analysis."

The amount of effort you put into managing your relationship with your wife/ex-wife/ex-girlfriend is going to be far less than the amount of time, trouble, and expense with which you just may find yourself saddled should that relationship go sour. Sometimes managing that relationship requires nothing more than counting to ten before answering a question. Other times it'll take a Herculean effort and hours and hours of talking.

Of course, if you're independently wealthy, don't need to work, have few friends and hobbies, and find yourself with more time and money than you need, you probably don't see any downside to making things difficult for the mother of your kids. On the other hand, how many of these men actually exist?

We'll discuss the myriad benefits of getting along with the mother of your children in more detail in Chapters 3 and 12.

Balance Work and Family

One important question that you, as a long-distance dad, must ask yourself is, "How do I successfully balance the needs of the workplace with the needs of my family?" Next, ask yourself how you will interact and bond with (smile at, talk to, play with, etc.) your child if you are separated from that child in those first few crucial months? Can an "absent" or long-distance dad be as good a father as a man who is "on the scene" day after day, working a nine-to-five job, sitting down to dinner with his child, showing up for all of that child's activities? Of course he can! There have always been long-distance dads, and long-distance dads today have it easier than those in the past. Due to advancements in technology, they have a better chance of being involved in their child's life than any of the long-distance dads of the past had.

Is an ever-present father really a realistic model? Can one say of that model that it is the only way to raise well-adjusted children? And what *is* the balance? Not only for "road warriors," but also for dads who are more or less "traditional fathers," what is that balance?

If you're in your twenties or thirties, you're probably going all-out to succeed, to establish yourself in a career. And since you've got a family to provide for, you've got that added pressure to do well in the workplace, get the promotion, bring home a greater financial stake to better provide for the family that you love, and so on. So again, you have to ask yourself, "How do I find that balance?" Is it possible to make that effort and, at the same time, be a loving and affectionate husband and father, one who is not distracted much of the time by the constant pull of work and the efforts required to earn a living? We'll discuss these and other questions in further detail in Chapter 4.

Build a Support Network

The question above about balancing parenting and work and other philosophical questions lie at the center of good parenting.

While the archetypal TV sitcom father is the inept, inattentive, and (literally) cartoonish Homer Simpson from *The Simpsons*, you don't have the luxury of being able to lie back and let your family life come to you. It is important at times like this to recall that while you may be living alone or as a single parent, you're certainly not alone in that.

Your church, synagogue, temple, or mosque can be a particular help to you in times of crisis, and even when you're feeling all right with your work-life balance, it's certainly not a bad idea to cultivate spiritual relationships that can reinforce your belief both in yourself and in something greater than yourself. If you're not comfortable with organized religion, there are other options as well, such as your local community center; community outreach organizations; the National Fatherhood Initiative; and fraternal organizations such as the Masons, the Elks, the Eagles, and so on. But it's tough to go this "alone" when you really do feel that way. We'll explore this subject further in Chapter 5.

The Most Important Thing—Commitment

What counts most in what you do for a living? Ability? Sure. Initiative? All right. Timeliness? Certainly. No less a sage than Woody Allen, that beacon of manliness, said, "80 percent of success is showing up."

And he was right, at least for the important role of fatherhood. Of course, "just showing up" demonstrates that most cardinal of fatherly virtues: *commitment*.

You can read all of the books in the world (including this one), take all of the courses, talk the best game, come up with engaging and innovative ideas for ways to gain and maintain meaningful time with your kids, but none of it will do you a lick of good without some *commitment* on your part. Commitment is the glue that holds together any solid relationship, especially during the rocky times. Since you're the adult in this relationship, it's incumbent on you to get the ball rolling, and to model for your kids what the word "commitment" really means. Sometimes it's as simple as literally just showing up. Sometimes it's not overreacting (or underreacting, for that matter) when the time comes to give your kid a consequence for having swiped twenty bucks from your wallet. Other times it's writing that college tuition check. Still other times it's taking them on that graduation vacation they've dreamed about for years.

Commitment takes involvement, and involvement, conversely, takes commitment.

2

Kids, Transitions, and Structure

STABILITY AND STRUCTURE ARE IMPORTANT IN the life of any child, regardless of his or her age. In fact, the need for stability and structure is second only to your child's need for your love, and constant reminders of that love. This chapter will discuss the different ways that kids need structure—from their parents, when learning that their dad will be gone, and when they spend time with you, either at their full-time home or at your house.

Explain the Time Spent Apart to Your Children

Explaining to children why Mom and Dad will be living apart is potentially very difficult and painful to all concerned. And it doesn't matter whether you're having this discussion with your children as a separated/divorced dad, as a road-warrior dad, or as a deployed dad. Children are not developmentally equipped to live anywhere other than in the moment, where consequences (such as discipline) are either immediate or simply don't occur. To them, a day can seem like a lifetime, and saying that Dad will be gone for only weeks/months/a year is usually going to have the same impact as saying that Dad is leaving for good. This is why when you have this talk with your kids, you must give it the same sort of effort and preparation that you would if you were discussing a permanent split.

It is a daunting experience because our children mean so much to us. The last thing we want to do is hurt or frighten our kids, and breaking the news to them does both. They need and deserve an explanation, and they have a right to know what to expect in their future. Fathers need to prepare themselves in order to explain the situation properly.

Taking the time necessary to understand what should and should not be said, and then rehearsing, will eliminate a lot of grief. To get a better understanding of what to say, you can pay for an hour of a counselor's time or speak with a capable father who has been through the process himself.

Bear in mind that preparation is the key here. Try to anticipate your children's questions, and try to be prepared for dealing with such inevitabilities as the first time your child is with you and says that she misses Mommy (phone calls are a godsend for dealing with that), or the first time she's at home and you're not and she says she misses you (with family calling plans, your child can have his or her own inexpensive cell phone that allows for unlimited talk time with both parents, for example).

Once a father knows what to say and how to say it, he needs to think about the proper place to communicate with his children. The privacy of home usually makes the most sense. Within the home, neutral places such as the living room, the kitchen table, or the back porch work well. These locations provide privacy and are nonthreatening. It is very important that you ensure that your family has privacy so everyone can feel it is safe to express their emotions.

Many fathers ask, "How much explaining should I do?" Depending on their age, children need to hear only those details that are appropriate and that directly affect their lives. Hearing the intimate details of their parents' lives can damage children. Every talk will be different, but an explanation—albeit overly simplistic—might sound something like this:

For a divorced or separated dad:
"We need to have a family talk. I'll talk first, and then it will be your turn. You know that your mother and I haven't been getting along . . . so we have decided it is best to get a divorce. This only means that she and I won't be living together. We still love you and both of us are always going to take care of you. We tried as hard as we could to live together and to be happy, but we can't. So in the future, you will have two homes: one at this house and one at your mom's."

For married dads who are leaving due to business or the military:
"I'm going to serve our country" or "I'm going to be here"— at which time you point to the place on the map where you'll be going—"for X number of days. I'll do whatever it takes to help us get through this. I want you to know that I love you and that I will always be here whenever possible, and even when I'm not here physically, I will be thinking of you. I plan to be back on [state the date] for [however long you'll be home]."

At this point in the conversation, give the children a chance to express themselves, indicating that it is safe for them to vent their feelings, whatever they are. Some may show their pain as anger, others may cry, and still others may end up showing no emotion at all.

Fathers can be certain their children are hurt. Ask them how they feel, hold them if they will let you. Let children know it's okay to cry or to say whatever is on their minds. At this time—especially at this moment—they need to know they matter. Taking the time to prepare, explaining appropriately and in a safe place, and then listening assures them that you care.

Children will draw their own conclusions about why you're leaving. Because of their inexperience, they lack understanding. Seldom will children consider how difficult divorce or one parent's having to leave is for their parents—and at times children may even seem insensitive. Bear in mind, no matter how the talk appears to be received, the family will have many painful feelings to deal with.

If you're divorcing, remember to hold your tongue if tempted to say something negative about your ex-spouse. This will limit conflict, help salve old wounds, and reassure the children that both parents will remain in the "family." This is a key step in preparing for the long reconstruction period, during which acceptance and healing must take place. As child counselor Claudia Alonzo says, "I don't think any parent should ever badmouth the other parent. And that is probably the hardest thing for parents not to do when they split up."

Children mainly want to know how the separation is going to affect them. They want assurances, as evidenced by good plans, that their lives will go on as normally as possible. Where there are unavoidable disruptions, they need to know that you will make that transition as smooth as you can for them. The parent's explanation should end with some open-ended questions designed to draw out the children's concerns or, at least, "Do you have any questions?"

Family Meetings

Family meetings are a must for the father who is going to be away for long periods of time. These can be casual gatherings. The father should think the meeting through beforehand and follow these tips:

- Meet in a place where people feel comfortable.
- Be sure the place is quiet so communication is possible.
- Make sure the place is a family-friendly environment so kids can be present.
- Keep the meeting to one hour so family members don't become tired and, in turn, emotional.
- Discuss details openly and directly.
- Remain in charge. This is your time to let people know what is happening with you.
- Tell those who matter to you that you love them.
- Tell them exactly when you expect to see them next.
- Tell them what life will look like then.

Gauge how much information to give your children based on how old they are and the type of relationship that you have with their mother. If you are divorced, make sure to explain to the children what differences they'll be experiencing in the upcoming weeks, but assure them that the changes will even out and things will become normal. Assure them that their parents will always be in their lives. It is best to tell them what the new family will look like and how it will operate, keeping the focus on how Mom and Dad are going to work together to still be their parents and be involved in their lives.

Structure Interactions with Your Kids

No matter what situation you're in, it will help your children remain positive if you structure every interaction that you have with them after you've become a long-distance dad. Nothing matters to your children more than knowing that you love them. Second is the sense of stability, and this comes from structure— a planned course of action—designed by the father, with his child's need for stability in mind.

No matter what age the child is, a father can instill in him or her a sense of stability by repeating the same routine each time father and child meet or when interacting with them from afar. If a child is an infant, the father's first words and touch (touching her cheek) may be the same each time the two of them meet, for example. Here are some more ideas:

- If his child is a toddler, the ritual might be: Dad lifts his child up above his head and asks, "Who is Daddy's favorite person in the entire world?" When those words are repeated every time father and child meet, that will become a fond memory, a reminder that he loves his child more than anyone, and something his kids can look forward to each time they see each other.
- For children who are older, say six or seven years of age, there may be a handshake or silly act that is to be expected. One father jokes with his son by holding out his hand to shake hands, and when the child reaches out to take his hand, the father pulls his hand back and runs his fingers through his

own hair. That is a joke that father and child play on each other and both enjoy it.

- For kids visiting their divorced father for the summer or Christmas break, there may be a ritual that signals the beginning of time spent with Father. Because this transition is a change from the child's regular schedule, there needs to be a ritual that begins the process of living with Dad. Joseph always goes grocery shopping with his children on the way to his/their home. Walking up and down the aisles selecting food and household items allows his children and him a relaxed time to prepare physically and emotionally for the children's time with Dad.

- For young adults, the ritual may include questions about the child's life. The questions need to be casual and not threatening, the parent inquiring as a friend would. The act of inquiring about the latest event, challenge, or adventure is the ritual; Dad's willingness to share in the excitement of the child's latest interest is what will produce the fond memories and the excitement of the child to greet and speak with Dad again.

- If your child has a regular event in his or her life that you cannot be at, make it a habit to consistently call him or her afterward. This could be calling after every soccer game to get a rundown of what happened, or after a dance recital to find out how all of the costumes turned out.

- You could mail your child a card of congratulations at the end of every semester of school. If you make sure to do this consistently, your child will come to rely on the gesture in a positive way.

No matter what you do, the key is to be consistent. Children don't expect parents to be perfect, but they do need consistency from you. If you do forget to do something, apologize quickly and let them know that you'll try your best to remember in the future. Taking these steps is important so everyone—kids, dad, mom, stepmom, ex—knows what to expect when you are together and when you are apart.

Limit the Opportunity for Misunderstandings

Communicate with everyone in a way that limits the opportunity for misunderstandings.

Communicating about Spending Time with Your Kids

Kids need ongoing casual reminders about what is going to take place when they see you. Send your kids a letter and mention a few things you want to do when the two of you get together. Ask them what they would like to do. Consider the kids before you make your suggestions: What are their interests? What might benefit them? How might you kill two birds with one stone by doing something that is both entertaining and educational? Follow up with a postcard to say, "Just thinking of you . . . and I'll see you in two weeks." Don't forget to be casual with your reminders and to listen to the tone of the children's voice. Their tone and words will let you know when and if you are mentioning the upcoming get-together too often.

Keeping Appointments

It is disturbing and emotionally painful to a child when a parent misses an appointment with him or her. Therefore, this is to be avoided at all costs (of both time and money). Be sure to write down the days and times when you will have the chance to be with your children. Know before you speak with the children's mother what times are available. If you don't live so far away that this is unrealistic, offer to watch the kids when you know their mom might be crunched for time. This is a bridge-building technique for divorced parents, and it is helpful for co-parents and even married folks. Allow yourself a day for transition between work and time spent with your kids. Give yourself some quiet time, some time to get ready, and some time to settle into the parent mode. If you go from a busy work schedule to one-on-one time with high-energy kids, you might be grumpy and not at your best when they are with you, so take a day to transition to dad mode.

Also mark on your calendar family events, children's ball games, recitals, and other special occasions just in case your schedule changes and you realize that you now have a window of opportunity to attend your child's T-ball game or dance recital. Be sure to let your child's mother know as soon as you are sure that you can drop in for a visit. She may have arrangements that might not work for you to be at an event, such as a new boyfriend meeting the kids for the first time. Be careful and respectful of her time with your children.

Remain Consistent in Your New Home

When you create a home away from your children, taking them into consideration might not be your biggest concern. There is the stress of finding a new location to live, selecting a house or apartment, filling it with furniture. However, it's well worth the effort to keep your kids in mind when you're doing all of those things, as they will (hopefully) be visiting often.

Kids Like It Clean

It is often money well spent to hire a house cleaner to put a shine on your home a day or two before your children arrive for an extended stay. There are a few reasons a house cleaning before the children arrive is a good idea.

1. Clean is important, as it tells the children that their visit to Dad is very special. In addition, if at all possible, children should have their space/place/room. Something that is always theirs and is always there waiting for them to return.
2. Some divorced mothers are looking for an excuse to cancel Dad's time with his kids, and a dirty living environment is sometimes used against a dad.
3. A clean house means that Dad can focus more of his time on his children instead of those dishes, the messy family room, or the children's rooms, which may not have been used in a month.
4. It is especially important to have the child's room organized and clean before the child arrives. A layer of dust on toys and books is a depressing sight and makes them unpleasant to play with.

As mentioned by Dr. Warren Farrell in the DVD *The Best Interests of the Child*, women's and girls' minds are different from men's and boys'. It is easier for a mother's mind to become bothered by details that men would not view as important. Knowing this, fathers can be on the lookout for details such as the child's room being dusty or dirty dishes in the sink—items that may trigger the mother's ire and give her issues to stew over. An ounce of prevention is better than a pound of cure.

Be Consistent When They Visit

Many long-distance dads try too hard to make up for the previous time away from their kids. Remember, your kids love you and are simply happy to be with you. Don't bring up the past, a missed appointment, or feelings of loneliness; basically, don't be a downer. Focus on today and this opportunity to enjoy the time you and the kids have together.

Try to plan ahead. One week before your children are scheduled to be with you, phone your children's local friends and set up some playtime. By phoning a week in advance, you allow enough time for your kids' friends' parents to schedule a time for the kids to get together, you demonstrate your parenting skill, and you and your kids have something fun to do so your mind is at ease knowing arrangements are made. Now you can relax and look forward to time spent with your kids.

Let the kids' mom know that you are aware of the upcoming time to be spent with your kids. Chances are she will be more aware of the coming date and a little uneasy about it. Put her mind at ease by reminding her that you are thinking of the upcoming date and making plans and that you are happy to include her in the planning. Mothers want both the best for their children and the assistance of their children's father, so reassure her by talking things over with her and remind her that you are capable of managing the situation when you and the children are together. Encourage her to let you take charge of part of the planning. For example, if the family is going to Yosemite for a camping trip, take responsibility for planning part or all of that trip. Remind Mom that she does not have to manage everything just because you are away. Despite your willingness to make the plans, however, mothers often feel a need to understand and manage family matters, so fill her in on the details. At the same time, encourage her to pass the reins to you and to relax. Demonstrate to your children and their mother that Dad can manage the family's needs.

Remember Important Dates

Be sure to have a calendar with the upcoming event in sight of the entire family, remind everyone of the event and date, and discuss details with the mother—all the while demonstrating your ability to plan things out and to prepare ahead of time for the big day or week.

Be sure to keep all the adults in your life informed. Fathers look bad and lose creditability when it is discovered that they did not have the ability to stay on top of a plan and did not remember the date, set things up to succeed, and inform the people involved. Keeping all informed can be the father's chance to show the world how capable a father he is.

If you're divorced, a calendar with the time the children are scheduled to spend with their father should be mailed to the ex (this makes a good gift on New Year's Day).

Remind her of upcoming time you have with the kids two months in advance.

Mention to her your commitment to support her in co-parenting and ask her to do the same for you.

Let Them Know What to Expect While You're Away

A long-distance father's job is to inform everyone of his schedule and how he will keep in contact while away. You can use a calendar, set up phone-call schedules, explain your travel or work, and set up virtual visitation. Details matter, so be sure everyone knows what to expect, and follow the time line you set up. If a situation, such as needing to carry out a military operation, means you miss a scheduled virtual visitation time, explain before you depart for overseas that this may happen. With the knowledge that "sometimes military dads are unable to phone home," your children now have an understanding of why the call was missed and, in turn, less of a sense of loss.

Explain what is involved in your business travel: thousands of travelers in major airports, foreign languages, foreign telephone services and phone numbers with thirteen numbers, time differences that may mean different days of the week, customs that differ compared to those in the United States. These topics all make interesting conversation for fathers and their kids and help educate children, giving them an understanding of what their father goes through just to connect with them while away.

Road-Warrior Dads

Michael Gough always shows his children parts of the cities where he is working. In San Francisco, Michael held his laptop computer with its virtual-visitation camera pointing to the Golden Gate Bridge, and showed his daughter Saige the bridge, a wall of sea fog, seagulls, and the rolling hills packed with colorful plaster houses. Digital pictures sent home by Dad can become screen savers for kids and reminders of places their father has been. Dads who can do so should show things that kids love doing, such as pictures of sailboats, soccer games, and train stations.

Deployed Dads

Soldiers need to be careful not to scare their children. It is interesting to hear about the 130° temperature on the Afghani airstrip or what you ate in a local cafe, but it is terrifying to hear about your landing at midnight with no landing-strip lights, no lights on the troop carrier, and all buildings blacked out so that the insurgents have less of a chance of killing the latest deployment of U.S. soldiers. The fact that you exited the plane at a full run in total darkness, wearing night-vision gear and rifle at the ready, paints a picture that can give your children nightmares. Someday your children will be better off with this knowledge, but for children whose fathers are still active, that information is a burden, not a gift.

Children are reassured by knowing that their military parents are well prepared, and some boys and girls enjoy hearing of the challenging training and drills. Children like the idea that their father is strong and capable of protecting himself, so the more knowledge that reassures children that their dad will return, the better. If there are postcards of your location, send one to your kids. Let them see the conditions around you, but leave out the scary things. Descriptions from a foreign country of children their own age and how these kids live differently from them are educational and interesting, and the fact that Dad is writing them demonstrates his love for his kids. Consider sending a unique gift to your kids—the more unique the gift, the better, and soldiers are often around unusual items. When you send back a cool present, encourage your child to speak about it with his or her friends. Why not show and tell about some local money?

Divorced Dads
Divorced fathers living a great distance from their children have an opportunity to include their children in "dad's life" in his town and state. Why not subscribe to the local newspaper

and have it delivered to your children and get the local newspaper in your children's hometown delivered to you? You both can keep up on local news in each other's town. Look for articles in your area that parallel things that interest your children. Once you find common ground to talk about, reinforce that connection with questions about your common topics. Show your kids that you are aware of what interests them in their town, and if that same topic is relevant in your town, share and compare the similarities and differences. This will make it easier for your child to visit you, because he or she will have an understanding of something in your town.

Also send souvenirs from your current or new town that relate to your children's interests. If your daughter is an aspiring dancer, send a schedule of dance troupes that will be performing in your town when your daughter is visiting.

When You Return

When long-distance dads return, there is often the urge to make up for lost time. Some fathers make the mistake of becoming a "Disney Land Dad"—they become entertainers committed to showing the kids a good time. Fast food, candy, and staying up late with Dad all seem like good ways to make up for time spent away from kids. Unfortunately there is a price to pay for that kind of fun. Kids revved up by sugar and poor eating habits can become tired and cranky and are no fun for anyone.

Being a good father requires setting boundaries for kids and enforcing those boundaries. When long-distance dads parent well, insist that kids eat well, get lots of rest, and remind the kids that even though dad was away for a long time there will be plenty of time to reconnect, fathers can remind their children that dad will do all he can to be in his kids' lives for the next fifty years or more.

Returning from Deployment

When you're a soldier, getting home safely is only half the battle. When fathers return after deployment, or before they arrive state side, they can seek the counsel of a marriage or family therapist or counselor to help prepare them to return to family life. Living in a battle zone where your peers protect you and you them is very different from being a father in a home in the United States. There is literature provided by all branches of the military to prepare fathers to return to civilian and family life.

Returning to one's home after a tour of duty during which time the wife or ex-wife has assumed the role of manager of family details can be challenging for both father and mother. Both must get used to sharing the decision making at a time when both must get used to each other's being in the house again. Time, counseling, and peer support all can contribute to a safe and steady adjustment. Discuss with your wife what you both expect to happen, and be realistic about the time needed to adjust to change.

When Kids Are the Ones Transitioning and Traveling

When children are moving from one home to another, it requires an adjustment period. Because children of divorce are always away from one of the two people they love most, those children are always missing one of their parents. When they are with Mom, they miss Dad, and when they are with Dad, they miss their mother. Many small children have nightmares because of this, which is disturbing to both parent and child. However, having the child at one home all the time does not make it easier for the child. What can divorced parents do to put their children's mind at ease when they're upset about being away from one parent or the other?

1. Remind the children that both parents love them.
2. Tell the children how long it will be before they can see the other parent.
3. Remain in charge; do not let the children dictate the parenting arrangement. Children lose a sense of security when they realize they can control their parents.
4. If a child cries and wants to return to the other home, remind the child that this is the time for you two to be together, and when it is time to be with her or his mother, you will make sure that happens.
5. Although listening to your child cry for his or her mother feels like it will break your heart, remember that the child is most likely doing the same for you at Mom's house.
6. Sit with your child and read with him or her. Keep physically close to your child and comfort him or her with gentle touches.
7. The very best thing to do when a child is missing his or her other parent is bring out materials to get the child involved in a high-interest activity; the more active the activity, the better.
8. Having a calendar with the days that your child will be with you and the days the child will be at Mom's house allows you to show your child how much time has been spent and how much time remains before going to Mom's house.

9. Be sure to make the child's room a fun place. Your child needs his or her own room. Make sure that room is a place your child likes. Spend time in the room with your child—remember that it is his or her special place, and you are adding to the fun of being in that room. Decorate the room with pictures of Mom, family, and you.

10. Always make a big deal about the child's room. Notice toys, books, school work, and so forth that the child enjoys. Your appreciation of his or her room adds to the specialness of that room. Invest in that room; it shows your child how much you value him or her.

The Challenges of Kids Traveling

One unfortunate side effect of being a long-distance dad is that when you and your children see each other, one or the other of you often must travel in order to do so. This might not be such an issue for you as an adult, but traveling is different for children, especially when they are doing it alone. Luckily, these days, the airlines have very good chaperoning practices in place to keep track of "unaccompanied minors," and they will make sure that children are handed off to the correct person upon arrival at the airport. If your child is nervous about traveling alone, walk him or her through the steps of exactly what will happen. It might even be beneficial for you to physically go through it with your child the first time so that he or she will be more comfortable when doing it on his or her own.

If you have the time and resources, you can follow Jerry's example. Every other Thursday, Jerry gets up at 5:00 A.M. and drives to San Jose, California, to board his flight to Seattle so he can meet up with three-and-a-half-year-old son Zachary at preschool. Together they ride a Yellow Cab to the airport and board the plane for their flight back to San Jose, California, then drive to Santa Cruz, arriving home at 9:00 P.M., just in time for bedtime at Zack's and his daddy's California house. Friday morning, Dad takes Zachary to preschool in Santa Cruz so that Jerry can put in eight hours of work.

"It takes a day's travel to get Zachary from Seattle to Santa Cruz. We do that every other week. It's pretty hard on him. We spend the weekend together, but we don't spend enough time in

---

Unaccompanied Minor Travel Tips

Take your child to the gate and wait there with him or her. Explain that his or her mother will be waiting at the other gate when the plane lands. Some airlines require parents to wait at the gate until the plane is in the air. This makes sense because occasionally planes have problems and flights are canceled.

Pack a backpack for your child and include what he or she might need to enjoy the flight. "Zack always has a backpack with his portable DVD player, two movies, head phones, a couple of books, snacks, and gum. The gum is a must; it helps his ears adjust to the pressure, which can be painful for young children," says dad Jerry.

When the plane arrives and you are to meet your child, sit at the gate and hear about the flight—don't debrief the kid, just ask about the flight and make small talk to allow time to adjust.

Phone ahead and explain to the airline that you wish to meet your child at the gate. Some airlines will issue you a noncomplete boarding pass that allows you to meet your child at the gate. You cannot board the plane, but you will be allowed past security and on to the gate where you will meet your child, accompanied by a flight attendant.

Santa Cruz to feel settled in. Zack has friends and family here and that is important to him, but it's hard on me because Monday morning we are off to the airport for half a day's travel for Zachary to return to Seattle and his mother, and a full day for me to get back home. Two days of travel, costing $1,500, for a weekend visit with his dad twice a month. It's worth it though, even for such a short amount of time."

Get Emotionally Reconnected with Your Child

It's good to have a routine you and your children do together that is a signal of the transition to time with Daddy or to Daddy's being back in the house.

Remember that the transition to time with Dad or Mom can be emotional for children. A quiet transition can be good, and something that includes an activity can also be helpful. The transition should be an enjoyable activity and one that is easy to arrange, such as a bicycle ride or a walk on the beach. You can include one or a couple of your children's friends if they voice a preference for that (not necessary for teenagers).

If you're a divorced father picking up your kids from their mom's house, it is a good idea (if you and your ex-wife are on speaking terms) to mention in a kind voice that you and your child will return in a certain number of days. For clarity, mention the place and time that the next exchange will occur. This reminds everyone of what to expect and provides a sense of security.

When a divorced father picks up his children for a visit, he should spend about fifteen minutes making small talk with his child's mother. This shows the child that his mother and father get along. It provides the child with time to gather last-minute things he or she may need, and it eliminates the sense that the child is just "a piece of luggage" transported from one place to another. The conversation that the father has with his child's mother is best if it is lighthearted and focused on the child; for example, a father might compliment the child on her new dress and give the mother kudos for selecting such a cute outfit. This brief interaction is a bridge-building opportunity and a conflict-management example the child can observe and choose to practice. The main goal for divorced parents is to have a sane exchange and to model for the children how people treat each other with respect.

I remember feeling sad that my daughter, Stephany, had to carry her suitcase from house to house, so I mentioned, "Stephany, I'm sorry that you have to travel back and forth every week." She replied, "Dad, this is the best of all the options."

It is sometimes debated whether children should have one home to live in for stability rather than switching between two. I have never heard that from a child. It appears that children would rather move than lose contact with one of their parents.

Your Behavior Is a Model

Long-distance dads have the opportunity to model for their children how one handles emotionally challenging situations. It is emotionally challenging to be a long-distance dad, no matter what the cause. Fathers love their children, and anything that means the father must leave his children and return a visitor presents an emotional challenge. Often, fathers who are long-distance dads feel a sense of loss, and that sadness can be expressed as anger toward the child's mother or toward life in general. Still, there is an opportunity here for long-distance dads to educate their children in self-control and commitment during life's challenging times.

3

Preparing to Be a Long-Distance Dad

AS WITH ANY OTHER LIFE-ALTERING TASK, LEARNing how to become the best long-distance dad you can possibly be is made all the more difficult by the question of where to begin. Here's your starting point: a set of guiding principles to keep in mind while cultivating a successful relationship with your kids. Some of them will work fine for you, others might not. They are intended as guidelines, not hard-and-fast rules for you to follow. (When it comes to parenting, there really are none of those, regardless of how much you may wish for them!) As such, if they work for you, keep them. If they don't, feel free to tweak them until they do.

GUIDING PRINCIPLES

1. Commit to your child's life. Convey, by work and deed, that you will stay connected.

2. Make clear that while there may be obstacles, financial or otherwise, your child can count on love and support.

Sometimes a dad has to say, "I'll do my best, but circumstances might prevent my attending every occasion—game, recital, holiday—that's important to you."

3. Most parents would love to have a perfect attendance record, but occasionally—*occasionally* being the critical word—things come up that get in the way.

4. Listen. One way to demonstrate the love you feel for your child is to listen to her. Listen with your whole being. What better way to communicate love and respect?

5. When a child realizes her words matter to Mom and Dad, it provides her with a sense of self-worth.

6. Listening well pays dividends. Listen well to your kids, and they, in turn, will likely listen to you.

7. Model for your children what good listening looks like. It's a skill, and it will serve them throughout their lives.

8. Apologize to your child when you are wrong. No one is expected to be perfect. Make that a house rule, and you and your children are off the hook. When you make a mistake, apologize and move on.

Separations are always difficult. With the more permanent (and more common) ones such as legal separation and divorce, the process of separating is often drawn out and painful. Even the briefer periods of separation from your kids such as those experienced by military fathers and road-warrior dads can be hard on both parents and children.

In this chapter we'll deal with how you can best prepare for the coming changes in your family's basic structure. We'll start with ways for you to address divorce, since that is the most common form of parental separation from children. However, we'll look at other forms of paternal separation, including brief or periodic work-related separations (for married road-warrior dads) and longer work-related separations (such as for married military dads deployed overseas).

Preparing for a Separation Due to Divorce

A marital breakup is usually bookended by two distinct periods of unrest in the home. First there is the period when the marriage is ending, characterized by arguments over everything from children to finances and back again. This is followed by the separation of the parents, which, in turn, is often followed by another period characterized by further bickering about many of the previous issues, in addition to such new wrinkles as access to the children and child support.

In the process, the sanctity of the home is often destroyed. A first priority of responsible parents is to do everything possible to rebuild that which their divorce has torn down. A new home must somehow be constructed on the foundation of the old one in order for both children and parents to feel secure. There is much to do, and time is of the essence.

As difficult and painful as it can be, there is a beginning, middle, and end to the process of restructuring the family. What's more, there is much a devoted father can do to help his children (and by association, himself) to heal.

For example, many fathers choose to improve the quality of their lives and the lives of their children by making a commitment to co-parent with their child's mother. Co-parenting provides both mother and father with multiple opportunities to provide for and protect their offspring.

Unfortunately, some men are understandably bitter following the breakup of their families. Thus, they are often anything but optimistic when someone suggests they engage in a co-parenting arrangement. Oddly enough, co-parenting is usually exactly what they need. Sharing their familial responsibilities allows both mothers and fathers the time and energy to successfully balance parenting, work, and solitude. And the children benefit even more from having both parents actively involved in their lives.

There are family counselors who oppose co-parenting out of the belief that moving children from home to home damages them. It takes a well-informed and determined man to successfully challenge these misguided (if well-intentioned) people. Such a man stands an excellent chance of helping to rebuild his family. The following sections explain how to progress from the grief and confusion that caring parents often feel following a break-up and move toward establishing a workable and healthy co-parenting relationship.

The Right to Parent

Donald T. Saposnek, Ph.D., and Chip Rose, J.D. (Doctor of Jurisprudence), C.F.L.S. (Certified Family Law Specialist), see in divorce litigation a process they call the "negative reconstruction of spousal identity." According to them, this is an all-too-common aspect of a relationship breakup where one spouse (or both) begins to actively think of the other in nothing but negative terms, and that this negative image is constantly reinforced every time the spouse either thinks about his or her partner or actively reflects on the marriage. In a nutshell, the spouse in question "rewrites marital history and selectively perceives only the events over the years that fit."

A father on the road to separation or divorce would do well to keep the above definition in mind while attempting to prepare both himself and his family for the changes on the horizon. The question is how to do this? How to be clear-eyed about this? Let's take a look at a checklist of questions you must answer, which I've prepared based on almost twenty years of working with divorced fathers, as well as on my own divorce:

- How can I re-establish myself as a father and parent of my children?
- How can I co-parent with my children's mother when we can't communicate?
- How can I protect myself against a legal system that casts me in the role of "Bad Guy" and demands more money of me than I can earn?
- How do I overcome the fear that I will not be allowed contact with my kids?
- How do I deal with an ex-wife who seems to want total control of the family?
- How do I deal with family law authorities who know little of my former mate or me, yet make decisions that have long-term affects on everyone involved?

There are no laws stating that fathers should accept anything short of a fair deal, yet every day uninformed men settle for less than they need to. Chip Rose, founder of the Mediation Center of Santa Cruz, California, attributes this to something called "rational discrimination." He says, "Today in the family law courts, there is a rational discrimination that favors women; (it) flows out of the natural allocations of labors that most couples create themselves. Mom gets pregnant, stops being functional (as a money-earner), stays at home, produces their child, and wants to be there to nurse. Dad is typically full of pride and wants his family protected, so he happily takes on all the income-earning responsibility."

Co-parenting Problems

Co-parenting problems can begin when mothers and fathers decide that only the mother-to-be should have a few months away from work before and after a child is born. Often there follows an agreement where the mother stays home for a few months more to nurse and care for the infant, while the father continues providing for his family. Many times men grudgingly agree to continue financially supporting the family well past the time when the mother could have gone back to work. A better option, seldom used by couples, is for both parents to spend equal time at home raising their children.

A history of shared parenting becomes very important in the event that a couple ever winds up divorced. Without that history, when a breakup occurs, the father will be expected to continue in his previously established role: that of breadwinner, carrying the income-earning responsibility whether his children live with him or not.

In California custody cases, for example, custody of the children is granted to their mother 80 percent of the time. This results almost exclusively from patterns couples establish while they're still married. When judges make rulings in custody cases, they're not generally interested in rocking the proverbial boat. They don't concern themselves with the question of whether the father is fit to be the primary custodial parent. Instead, they look at earning patterns in the household and attempt to keep the issues of support similar to those already established. In other words, the mother will usually get custody in a divorce settlement because she's already established herself as the primary caregiver, and the father will wind up paying support because in so doing, he'll also be continuing in his own established role.

Legally, fathers and mothers are expected to share the responsibility of raising their kids. Neither parent has the moral or legal right to coerce the other away from their children. Unfortunately, fathers are often forced out of the family. This is especially common in the first year or two after their divorce.

To protect yourself and your children during this difficult time, it is essential that you do everything you can to make clear your commitment to your family. At the same time, you must demonstrate your ability to practice emotional self-control as the courts often use it as a measure of your emotional maturity. In word and in deed, you, the father, must make it clear to the court that you want to remain an involved parent.

You're bound to be happier when thinking of your kids than when you are anguishing over your former spouse. The mere fact of your child's presence in your life, with its attendant need for structure, routine, and attention, goes a long way toward

Dad-to-Dad

These days, the overwhelming majority (75–90 percent) of marriages that wind up in divorce court do not end by mutual consent. Seventy percent of the time, it's the woman who wants out of the marriage, while the man wants to stay married. The partner who wants to leave the marriage tends to have already made his or her emotional peace with the end of the marriage before he or she has even filed for divorce. In other words, the spouse who didn't originally seek the divorce is likely to be caught emotionally as well as financially unprepared for the divorce process when his or her partner files.

keeping you engaged in the present, rather than brooding over the past or fretting over the future.

As a responsible father, you face something of a balancing act while working out the custody agreement with your lawyer, your ex's lawyer, and, frequently, with a judge. While demonstrating your absolute commitment to your children and the emotional bond that you share with them, you also must be careful to maintain at least outward control of your emotions, including your temper. This is without question the best way for you to make clear to the court not only that you *want* to remain an involved parent, but that it is in keeping with the all-important previously established family routine.

Your First Steps and Some Success Stories

Your first step in all of this is to get into the habit of demonstrating your competence to raise your children right alongside your ex-wife. It's generally agreed that the first six months following a breakup are the most difficult. Your actions during this emotional time are almost guaranteed to be revisited during later custody negotiations.

Good Dads DO

If you really wish to co-parent equally with your ex-wife over the long-term (regardless of the physical distance between your two homes), it's in your best interest to keep accurate records (through journaling, financial receipts, etc.) of the events subsequent to your initial separation from your wife. These detailed accounts can serve as proof of your ability to parent and as a defense against potentially negative allegations raised by your spouse during what can often be acrimonious custody discussions.

During this important time, you, as a father, must find ways to cope that don't include emotional outbursts directed at your spouse or your children. After all, it's perfectly natural for a man going through a divorce to experience anger, humiliation, and fear. Most feel unprepared, unprotected, and financially insecure—even suicidal. Men under emotional pressure from these sorts of feelings often (understandably) overreact to stress, such as that experienced during the process of breaking up a family.

Those of us who have been through the breakup of a family know how important it is to reach out to people for understanding. However, the last thing single fathers need is to be criticized, labeled, or included in someone else's preconceived ideas of what will and won't work for them. A competent, compassionate counselor can be very helpful, as can other fathers who have had experiences similar to those of a new single father.

Ask for Help

As a man, you're likely to find that self-reliance can often be an obstacle for you. There are two very good reasons why you should not attempt to rebuild your family all by yourself: first, everything done in the early days of divorce greatly influences what happens later, so it is important to get off on the right foot, and second, good choices early on can save you hundreds of hours of struggle and thousands of dollars in the long run. This is time and money that could be spent helping your family adjust to shared parenting.

Jim is a thirty-eight-year-old electrician and father who is still in the process of correcting his mistakes after five years. "Things got off to a bad start," he says. "I fell into disfavor with the judge because I was completely ignorant of family law." Jim's attempt to represent himself in his child custody battle failed miserably;

his past legal experience was not sufficient to establish a joint-parenting arrangement. (For more information on family law, see Appendix C.)

When David, a financial adviser for a small firm in California, was going through his divorce, he and his ex-wife used attorneys to battle it out. His wife told him that she was not only leaving him but taking their young daughter with her to England, and he was devastated. The first thing that he did was come to the Divorced Fathers Network, where we helped him figure out if there was any way to stop her from leaving (there wasn't) or if it was even best to try to stop her (in his case it was not in the family's best interest to have a big custody battle). In the network, he was able to learn from other fathers how to improve his relationship with his child's mother and educate her on how important a father is in the process of raising a healthy daughter. David set up a plan that included flying to England to spend time with his daughter at the mother's family's farm. This gave him the opportunity to establish cooperation with his ex-wife. Now she's come back to the United States, and their ability to communicate is such that he's relocating so that he'll be only half an hour's drive from his daughter. The whole process has taken five years. "All of this was directly possible because of what I learned from other fathers and their support," he says.

Talking with other divorced fathers about what lies ahead for you can be challenging at first. As one father put it, "I was afraid to reach out because men are supposed to be able to stand on their own two feet." Another remarked, "I had not been taught how to ask for support."

But although men have been taught to be self-reliant, bear in mind that this is the twenty-first century, the age of networking. Many men who are successfully co-parenting today regularly speak with other fathers. Generally, the people who set up co-parenting arrangements and remain involved with their children enjoy helping others do the same. Caring fathers can be a motivational force for you and serve as role models while you're working to figure out how best to co-parent.

He Says

Greg is a general building contractor in his late thirties who has been raising his daughters in conjunction with his former wife for the past five years. When she filed for divorce, he grabbed the phone book, looked under *Churches*, phoned, and asked for a counseling pastor. That call provided him with the opportunity to meet people who would help. He walked in to his first church-sponsored divorce recovery group and nervously joked, "Hi, have you got anything for a clueless guy like me?" From that moment on, he says, his life began to change for the better. "I felt I was safe. The people knew how I felt, and they wanted to help."

Your starting point for getting help is to first realize that you are *not* alone in this. Some men start with churches, but you can also usually find support by contacting other benevolent associations (the American Red Cross, the Society of St. Vincent DePaul, the Salvation Army, for example), or even by phoning counselors in your local community. Fraternal orders such as the Odd Fellows, the Knights of Columbus, the Moose, the Eagles, the Elks, the Masons, and the Shriners can also be counted on as a great starting point. If you're a veteran, don't count out such associations as the Veterans of Foreign Wars or the American Legion as sources of support. There are also organizations such as Big Brothers, the Divorced Fathers Network, and Parents Without Partners (see Appendix A for Web sites) that were founded specifically to help support parents in your position. Some men go so far as to start their own support networks by phoning each other on a regular "as needed" or "friendship" basis. The important thing is for single fathers not to isolate themselves and deny themselves the valuable resources that may be just a phone call away.

Preparing to Be a Married Road-Warrior Dad

OK, so you're headed toward a period spent as a long-distance dad, but it's not because you're getting divorced. There are a few things you can do that will help prepare both you and your children for your extended absence(s).

First and foremost, you must communicate, communicate, communicate. Not just with your kids, but with your wife! She's your partner in this, and she's going to be doing the lion's share of the parenting while you're away from your family.

Next, bear in mind that children (and by association, families) crave structure and thrive on routine. And since kids have no other true frame of reference for what is and is not "normal" in their home life, establishing a routine that can be carried out easily and with a minimum of fuss while you're away will save you and your spouse a lot of trouble while also going a long way toward minimizing your collective stress over the long run! So, the important thing is knowing where, when, and how to start!

You can also take heart from the fact that we live in an age where technology is making the world smaller with each passing nanosecond. For your older kids, there's the phone, e-mail, even chat programs such as those provided by online services such as Yahoo!, MSN, and AOL. Even younger kids, who might only just be learning to write or are possibly too young to even know their ABCs, can interact with you, the father, via things like webcams, a "Dad Board" on the back of your kid's door, and room decoration with an eye toward keeping Dad foremost in your child's mind and heart. We will explore more deeply these and other means that you can use to forge and maintain that special bond with your kids while you're away from them in succeeding chapters.

Preparing to Be a Deployed Dad

Although in many ways military fathers deployed overseas are the ultimate "road warriors," their situation and that of their families is distinctive enough that it merits its own section in this chapter on how to prepare for your time as a long-distance dad. We will deal with the actuality of being a deployed dad in succeeding chapters, including how to maintain and reinforce your bond with your kids, but in this section, we will talk about concrete ways to prepare yourself for your coming extended absence from your family.

Now more than ever, with fathers in both the active armed forces and the National Guard/reserves being deployed and redeployed overseas for multiple tours, you need to focus on making as sure as you can that your family will successfully weather the expense, loneliness, and outright stress involved in such a lengthy parting. Let's face it, if you're overseas defending your country, and you're stressed out about how the family's going to make ends meet back home, you're placing undue stress both on yourself and your wife, to say nothing of what your kids will no doubt pick up on.

Guidelines for Managing Your Money
While You're Deployed

So, let's start with managing your money. You're an adult, a breadwinner, and as such, you, or your wife (or hopefully, both), realize how quickly bills and "unforeseen expenses" like say the transmission goes out on the car, a child needs braces, or the furnace breaks, can eat right through the money you're making every month. Also, if you're a member of the National Guard or reserves, you're now possibly taking a considerable pay cut by leaving behind your civilian job for a year when you deploy overseas. All the more reason to get and keep your finances in as good a shape as possible. Here are some simple rules you can use to help tame your finances and keep them manageable while you're overseas:

One person pays the bills.

A simple enough rule, right? And while it might seem like conventional wisdom that the parent (in your case, your wife) who is not deployed should be the one paying the bills, this is not necessarily the case. Let's face it: if your wife is tending the kids, possibly also working part-time or full-time in order to help keep the family's collective heads above water, paying the bills could be just one more thing she has to shoulder in an otherwise very full schedule.

Here once again is where the wonders of technology can help you defray your wife's responsibilities, because most bills can be paid online these days, and most all forward-deployed U.S. armed forces have frequent Internet access. So it's possible for you to take that on, if your wife is willing to let you (not necessarily a foregone conclusion). Whatever you decide to do in this case, make sure that you discuss it thoroughly with your wife, and that you two come to the conclusion together (a rule of thumb that is an excellent one to keep in mind as a guiding principle for your marriage in general). You also ought to bear in mind that this guideline is an implicit part of all of the tips we're going over here.

Come up with a budget and stick to it.

Easier said than done, what with the way those "unforeseen expenses" can leap out at you in the middle of any given pay period! As with the guideline above, this is something on which you ought to collaborate with your wife. Make sure that you include every one of your recurring monthly bills. Also, when those aforementioned unforeseen expenses (think "auto repair") arise, it helps to have a contingency fund, which allows you to meet those expenses without putting your family in the poorhouse. Also, don't forget to budget for the costs of remaining as connected as possible with your family during your deployment. After all, things like international long-distance phone cards don't grow on trees.

Manage your credit cards or they'll manage you.

Remember: a line of credit is not your money. It's money that someone else is willing to loan you at an average of 20 percent interest. While it's true that credit cards can be a good source of ready cash in case of emergencies, a good rule of thumb for deploying dads where credit cards are concerned is that if you don't need it, cancel it. It's better than paying a minimum balance every month on something you can't really justify keeping while you're overseas.

It might also be a good idea for you to give your credit card companies a call before you deploy. Many companies have different rules for use in different countries, hefty (and often hidden) service and ATM fees, and some even have different cards they offer for use in different regions of the globe. Globalization might be making the world smaller, but it's not that small yet, and despite VISA and MasterCard's assurances, they're *not* always "everywhere you want to be" (assuming that you even want to be deployed in the first place, which for many deployed dads is a mighty big assumption!).

Maintain two separate checking accounts.

Perhaps you've had a joint account for years. Perhaps you already maintain separate accounts (say, for household expenses or the mortgage, and so on). Wherever you fall on this question, if you haven't already opened a separate account for your (the deployed dad's) use while you're away, this is something to which you and your wife should give serious consideration. After all, when you're living on one continent, in a radically different time zone, with the potential for the deposits and withdrawals from two people separated by thousands of miles to get so easily messed up, it's a good idea to keep these accounts separate to avoid the potential for things like NSF (bankerese for "Non-Sufficient Funds") fees.

Guidelines for Managing Your Family's Health Care While You're Deployed

As with managing money, health insurance is something that needs to be dealt with before you deploy. The stress of being overseas is enough to have to deal with, so it's important that you're not also worried about your family's health-care needs. Here are four guidelines for managing your family's health care while you're deployed.

Make the most of TRICARE and TRICARE Prime.

What is TRICARE? It's the U.S. military's health plan for servicepeople on active duty, and it also covers their dependents. If you're not enrolled in TRICARE, you're passing up one of the most important resources you will have in making your deployment overseas as painless as possible for you and your family: access to free (or greatly reduced cost) health care. If you're not enrolled in TRICARE, it's easy to get enrolled, once you've registered in the Defense Enrollment Eligibility Reporting System (DEERS), which you'd do on base, not with your primary healthcare provider. TRICARE Prime is a managed-care option that the Department of Defense offers to military families willing to enroll in it for a minimum of one year. This sort of managed care allows you to select a physician/cooperative from a DOD-approved list of Primary Care Managers (PCM), who will, in turn, manage your family's health care and bill the Department of Defense for the lion's share of the cost. You can find much more information about both of these programs online at *www. tricare.mil/*.

Keep close track of your and your family's TRICARE Prime identification cards.

Seems like a no-brainer, but you'd be surprised how many people don't do this. Make sure you know where you leave them, then make sure you leave them where you know you were supposed to leave them.

Record the TRICARE telephone number and keep it available.

Another apparent no-brainer; just make sure you do it. Don't just trust that you'll be able to find this number/information stored in your cell phone when the time comes. Cell phones break, get stolen, get lost, etc. Having this information in more than one spot is one way to allow for the potential of that happening. It's also a good idea to keep a photocopy of your family's identification cards and health and dental information, just in case the originals should get lost.

Make use of emergency services.

One of the great things about TRICARE is that you don't have to worry about whether whatever is ailing you will be covered should you need to go to any hospital's emergency room. This is not the case with most managed-care health plans, which will cover some things, won't cover others, and insist that if you *can* make it to whatever clinic they might have within a few hundred miles of you, that you *should* be able to make it there, or pay the complete cost of going to the emergency room out of your own pocket. Now how is that for a nice military benefit?

Guidelines for Managing Your Family's Legal Needs While You're Deployed

Nobody wants to talk to a lawyer until about half an hour after they really should have. If you're going overseas, it would be foolhardy for you not to take a few quick and easy steps to make sure that your family is covered in the event that you or they will have to deal with the legal system while you're gone.

Create and maintain a Family Care Plan.

Your Family Care Plan (FCP) ought to designate who among your dependents, relatives, or friends is your designated decision maker, both for the short and the long term. FCPs are required for many military personnel, but even if you don't fall into a category where they're required (such as military personnel married to military personnel, single parents, or your spouse requiring special care, such as maternity care, while you're overseas), an FCP is a great idea. It can only assist your designee (usually your wife) in making the tough medical, financial, and legal decisions that will need to be made while you're deployed. This plan should include at the minimum: a "power of attorney" (see below), your medical and dental information, and any appropriately specific instructions regarding how you would like your family business to be conducted while you're gone.

Draw up a power of attorney.

You may be asking, "Just what is a power of attorney?" A power of attorney is a legal document that empowers someone else to sign other legal documents (bills of sale; loans requiring a signature, such as car and house loans, for example) in your name. Another potential use for a power of attorney is empowering your child's babysitter or day-care provider to make emergency medical decisions on your child's behalf. These are very useful instruments, and are relatively easy to draw up. For more information on "powers of attorney" and a template of how to draw one up, visit either *www.bbean.com/power.htm* or *http://financialplan.about.com/cs/powersofattorney/index.htm*.

Make sure that you have a current will.

As with other times when you might need to speak to a lawyer, few people want to think about a will until after it's too late. If you die without a will, the state will consider you "intestate" and can intervene in your family's dispersal of your worldly possessions, even possibly charging a fee for doing so. Realistically, it's your stuff; don't you think you ought to be able to say who gets what and how much of it they get? As with a power of attorney, a will is fairly easy for you to draw up on your own. For more information, visit *www.legacywriter.com* or *http://LegalZoom .com/*.

Get a safe-deposit box for copies of these and all of your other legal, financial, and medical documents.

This ought to be self-explanatory. If you don't want to invest in a safe-deposit box, a home-stored fireproof lockbox is a possible alternative.

A Great Start!

If you've waded through the above guidelines and begun the processes entailed within them, congratulations, you're already far better prepared than over 50 percent of our armed service personnel currently deployed overseas! There are other tangible things you can (and should) do to prepare your family for your deployment overseas, including making contingency lists (what to do if your pet gets sick, what to do if the house is suddenly without water). We have provided several templates of these sorts of lists in Appendix B of this book. I don't doubt that you will find them very helpful. Lastly, thank you for serving our country, for the sacrifices you're making, and for protecting all of our children.

4

Successfully Balancing Work and Family

IT USED TO BE THAT WORK WAS THE ONLY MEAsure of a man. Fortunately, today, more and more men are valued for the love, tutoring, and security—both financial and emotional—that they provide for their children, wives, and families. But not everyone supports men in focusing more on the emotional needs of their family and less on work output. There are those who still believe men are made primarily to work. Bosses still want deadlines met, wives and ex-wives want more money in the bank account, and children want the latest advertised item. Men, too, push themselves to provide more financially. We often gauge our self-worth by what we produce, and we judge ourselves against other men's abilities. Many men are raised in communities where "big" men were those who earned the most.

Today more than ever before men are making time spent with their families a priority. For example, the fastest-growing family group in the United States is single-parent families headed by fathers. As it becomes socially acceptable for women to choose work over parenting, it becomes acceptable for fathers to pick time with their kids over time at work. Still, it is not easy for dads to limit their work hours so they can spend more time with their kids. I believe it is especially difficult for long-distance dads to manage their time and to prioritize parenting time above work and duty.

The Benefits of More Parenting

The benefit to those who parent more than they work is additional love-filled hours with their kids, walks in the park pushing a stroller, warm afternoons at the beach, camping in the woods, and time spent in the presence of our children's laughter. Dads who spend time with their children have a better understanding of who their kids are. Long-distance dads who do balance time spent with their kids and their responsibilities to work and military enjoy a sense within themselves that life is full and in order. The opportunity for fathers to take pride in time spent with their family has never been greater.

Philip is a recently divorced father. His ex-wife moved to Hawaii with their ten-year-old son, Josh, who spends the majority of time with his mom on the island. On the mainland, Philip stays busy creating and fitting custom doors for homes and businesses. His work is specialized and is in high demand in the affluent areas of California. Hawaii has little need for carpentry of Philip's level. The distance between him and his son was an obstacle that needed to be managed. How might a carpenter afford extended visits with his son and not fall into financial trouble? To spend more time with Josh, Philip finds home remodeling jobs on the island that allow him to live in the house while he remodels it. Philip can spend more time with his son by trading his work for room and board; the home owner gets an exceptional craftsman at a handyman's price, and Josh spends time with his dad, observing a hardworking father doing what is necessary to remain in his son's life.

Philip's child support obligation is based on his earning abilities on the mainland. To maintain his child support, Philip must work in California. The occasional remodeling job in trade for room and board is simply a way to spend more time with his son. Fortunately, it is one way for Josh to see and learn from his father.

Parenting Statistics

Take a look at the following statistics from the U.S. Department of Health and Human Services:

- Single fathers who work less than full time: 10.2 percent
- Single mothers who work less than full time: 66.2 percent
- Custodial fathers who receive a support award: 29.9 percent
- Custodial mothers who receive a support award: 79.9 percent
- Single fathers who work more than 44 hours per week: 24.5 percent
- Single mothers who work more than 44 hours per week: 7.0 percent

They're quite sobering, aren't they? The plain, cold, unvarnished truth is that when it comes to attempting to achieve what such top employers as Microsoft refer to as "work/life balance," a single father has many obstacles standing in his way. Some are economic, others are societal, still others are some combination of both. Add to that the fact that there are 1.1 million kids with parents on active duty, and you've got a lot of kids who are, for one reason or another, away from their father.

For many single parents it's a struggle to earn enough to pay the bills each month. Earning the money to pay for shelter, groceries, and the ever-increasing needs of maturing children can eat up more and more time. Still, divorced parents expect each other to do everything possible to financially and, at the same time, emotionally meet their children's needs.

We all know what terrific motivators kids can be. There may be nothing fathers love more than being viewed by their children as the loving provider. Whether their kids are living with them or not, dads dread having to say, "Sorry, I just can't afford it."

Avoiding the Trap of Materialism

Materialism is another thing driving men to work long hours. Although for some, long hours are part of their job, others are motivated to work long hours by the ego-pleasing sense of success provided by the grand homes, exotic cars, glamorous women, comfortable retirement, and envious subordinates those hours afford. For such men, prosperity is often nothing but a poor substitute for the family life they lost when their marriage went south. Those who are preoccupied with the material risk having things instead of relationships as monuments to their fatherhood. Everyone knows at least one divorced guy who is helping make this a truism and not just a cliché.

Groomed from birth to fill the provider role as we are, for many of us, our self-esteem is often dependent on our ability to provide financially for our families. Plenty of fathers may choose to put all their available time and energy into work in place of parenting. When this happens, it's the kids who suffer.

Your wives/exes/girlfriends will sometimes misconstrue your drive to work as insensitivity to the needs of your children. When it appears to a mother that earning money takes priority over the emotional needs of her children, that their father (you) is intentionally denying them his company, then conflict is likely. First, she feels sorry for her children; then she begins to resent *you*.

The Dangers of Making Work Your Top Priority

When you make work your top priority, you may just set in motion a process with a predictable outcome. Your children experience a sense of loss, which in turn makes the mother's life more difficult.

For those of us men who grew up being force-fed the attitude of "work first, family second," materialism can seem to be a part of our being. If this description fits you, it might be helpful to start trying to come to grips with this sort of values-based programming received since childhood. It will also likely make it easier for you to prioritize parenting and working.

He Says

"As a kid I had this low self-worth. I didn't think much of myself. As I grew older, my self-esteem started coming from my ability to work. Eventually, if I wasn't working I felt as if I was doing something wrong. The idea that work is all-important was drummed into me. In a nutshell, I was taught that I had worth only when I produced."—Michael B., long-distance father of Dylan

---

For many, the pattern of long days at work leads to their spouse's belief that the children are better off with her. For example, a wife can (understandably) feel resentful when her husband does not pay attention to her or his children. If the lack of attention persists, the pair often divorces. If he then does not visit his children regularly, she may decide not to honor his relationship with his children. It's a simple progression.

Julie is thirty-two years of age. She is a second-generation New Yorker. Her son Stewart is ten years of age. He seldom leaves his mother's side. Eight years ago the two of them moved to California, where she remarried and completed her master's program in music theory. She summed up Stewart's relationship with his father in words that might seem familiar to far too many of you (see "She Says" sidebar).

She Says

"Sure, William is a good provider, but if he had put one half of the energy into his son that he expends every day at the office, everyone would have been happier. When William and I separated, I was willing to stay in the New York area so that Stewart could have a relationship with his father. But when William chose work over his own son time and time again, I decided to start anew in California."
—Julie, mother of Stewart

To Julie, William's willingness to work instead of parent justified her moving to California. By staying in New York, she placed her child's relationship with his father ahead of her desire to move to California. As the custodial parent of Stewart, she has the legal right to move at any time. William's lack of understanding of his wife's right to move with their son, his lack of appreciation of her willingness to stay in New York, and his inability to parent more and work less allowed his ex-wife to change her priorities. I have witnessed this situation dozens of times. What typically follows is that William's relationship with his ex-wife continues to change. Because William is now 2,000 miles away from his son, the parents' discussions begin to focus less on the time father and son spend together and more on money, typically child-support payments. Most fathers in William's situation tend to blame their ex-wives; some invest time and money in legal battles trying to prevent them from moving away with the children. Dads generally lose these fights due to the lack of time they previously spent with their kids. The judges generally see no reason why the child should remain if the father makes work a priority over parenting. When a father's child leaves town, the father suffers the loss of a loved one. The best way to avoid having the children's mother move away with them, and in turn stay happier, is to spend time with one's children.

Putting Children's Needs First

The decision to parent more and work less is seldom easy, especially for men. Surrendering your financial ambitions to satisfy the emotional needs of your kids will often require you to first challenge, then change some of your core beliefs and the manner in which you measure your self-worth. Fortunately, many mothers prefer men who are good fathers to those who are great providers. Most men making the change to involved parenting find that they need the encouragement and help of friends and family if they are to avoid the old pattern of working sixty-hour weeks and spending a few hours with their children.

Fathers who ask family and friends to assist them in being more involved parents may find themselves deluged with invitations to participate in outings and holidays. Experiences of that kind may serve as gentle reminders that many of life's pleasures feel better than the sense of success that fathers get from earning money. Without the assistance of friends and family, many men fall back into familiar roles, and when the old work patterns recur, even the best long-distance parenting arrangements can begin to break down.

Temptations of the road (for instance, drinking and carousing) can also negatively affect parenting arrangements and can cause you to get sidelined and miss phone calls or other scheduled contact with your children. The stress of being deployed and the unavailability of resources such as phones can cause fathers to miss appointments and have a negative tone in their voice, which can confuse a child. Explain this in a word or two to the child by saying, "Forgive me if I sound cranky." It's OK to let kids know what you're going through without emotionally dumping on them.

Couple these challenges with the difficulty of maintaining a presence in your child's life without the daily routine of coming home, walking through the door, asking what's for dinner, and bending down to hug your children, and you've got a daunting task before you. Being part of your kid's life when you're a long-distance dad requires more conscious choice on your part, and more conscious effort, for that matter. After all, frequent scheduled phone calls and e-mails take more time and effort than daily dinner conversation does.

We will revisit the importance of building a support network in Chapter 5.

Working Less and Why It Can Be Worth the Trade-Off

Limiting the number of hours at the office can cause tension with fellow employees who work full-time. People who choose to work fewer than forty hours per week appear to some to be in conflict with what corporate America values most—dedication to the job, at times to the exclusion of everything else. Fathers who limit their on-the-job hours are generally valued less as employees than are men who are willing to pour most of their time into their job.

Jason Lauer is a long-distance dad and is also in charge of hiring for one of the Fortune 500 companies located in the heart of California's Silicon Valley. "Generally, in the corporate world, you risk being regarded as unmotivated if you are a father who puts parenting ahead of work," Jason says. "Unless you're willing to work your way up the ladder, you might find yourself moving toward the exit door. In Silicon Valley there is not much support for people who say, 'I just want the minimum number of hours. I'm going to stay right here until my kids are raised.' Most employers want to see motivated employees. People who are willing to put in long hours if need be. This can be a problem for parents who want to spend more time with their children and less time on the job. With some companies the attitude is, if you are not going for the promotion, you are apt to be replaced."

Jason goes on to say, "There are exceptions to inflexible companies and the hard-nosed bosses. I've hired parents who needed flexible hours and schedules that allow for time with children. Typically those parents are very appreciative and ideal employees. One man who comes to mind works three 10-hour days twice a month instead of a forty-hour week and that allows him two days for travel to drive the distance he has to go to see his children for weekend visits. He lives in the Silicon

Valley because that allows him to earn the amount of money he needs."

Long-distance dads don't want to be laid off and passed up for promotions. Many are already financially strapped. The consequences of turning down work—being fired—is especially frightening to parents who must live on meager budgets. Many are painfully aware that they and their children are only a paycheck away from homelessness.

On top of that, it's not uncommon for single parents moving laterally in the workforce to find themselves competing with a line of people with few or no family commitments who are only too happy to work sixty-hour weeks. Almost all long-distance parents could use the money that a full week's work generates, yet many, in order to parent better, choose to work a modified schedule or part-time.

Making Parenting a Priority

Tom, a long-distance dad from Santa Cruz, California, has two kids. Ryan, fifteen, and Sara, thirteen. After school both attend dance and acting classes. They need less of their dad's supervision now than they did when they were younger and spent little time at school. Since Tom is needed less at home, he recently moved on to a full-time position as a building inspector.

"I would encourage any father to consider working less," Tom says. "Especially if his children are under ten years of age. When they are little they want you to be home when school is out. They look forward to a hug and time with dad. As kids grow more independent, like when a teenager's friends become all important to them, then parents can work more. It's pretty simple." On top of that, most long-distance dads get what time they do get with their kids in blocks (summer vacations, time in between road trips or deployments, etc.), so it's not as if they can even just say, "I'd like every other Wednesday off," because they won't necessarily be around their kids every other Wednesday.

It's up to you whether you view this as a challenge or as an opportunity. After all, if you get your time with your kids mostly during school vacations, it wouldn't be that uncommon in today's family-friendly workplace for you to:

- Work extra when you don't have your kids
- Telecommute from home
- Take your kids to work with you

These are options that you should be exploring, and they're over and above the obvious choice: vacation time.

Reassuring Your Spouse or Ex-Wife about Income

Many current and ex-wives become alarmed that their monetary support will be reduced once they hear that the fathers of their children will be working fewer than forty hours per week. Your spouse, current or former, needs to be reassured that you intend to continue to assist her financially but that you intend to be physically present when the children are young and need two parents the most. Diplomacy on your part, employed early and often, can do a lot in terms of limiting conflict between you and her, and, if you're divorced, in avoiding trips to court.

When frightened, some divorced women may call the Family Law department responsible for collecting child-support payments (this department varies from state to state), hoping to maintain the previous level of support. Unfortunately, those in that office are not in the "cooperative parenting" business. While many of their staff understand and support the idea of shared parenting, their primary job is to collect child support. When the department of child-support services becomes involved, the parents' relationship can deteriorate.

Changing the Child-Support Arrangements When You Work Less

If your plan is to work less in order to spend more time with your children and that will cause you to earn less, always explain that goal—the intention to share in the job of raising the children—to your children's mother. This will reassure her that your intentions are honorable and that she will continue to receive financial support.

Child support is based on the father's past income. When the courts are calculating child support, judges usually want to see Dad's last three years' tax forms, pay stubs for the previous six months, and a recent profit-and-loss statement. When a father starts earning less, it becomes harder for him to make his payments because the court-ordered payment is not automatically lowered to match his income. It would be easier to work less and parent more if courts and the district attorney (DA)'s office responded quickly to changes in a father's income. Unfortunately, due to the amount of time that the legal process requires for modifications, typically six months to one year, many fathers who are working less in order to parent more appear to be behind in child support. When pre-existing support orders cannot be met because support payments do not accurately reflect the current income, Dad may appear to be a deadbeat, which may cause judges and the DA's office to view him with contempt.

To prevent such misunderstandings, a father can qualify his decision by placing in his case folder a letter that states (a) his intention to maintain a cooperative relationship with his children's mother, (b) his income and expenses as well as the updated support amount, and (c) his commitment to fulfill child-support obligations.

When the DA's office gets involved in a financial dispute, any progress the father may have made toward working less and parenting more generally comes to a halt. According to Kimberly Mel, as quoted when she was the assistant DA (ADA), Family Law Department: "The problem is that we have a small staff overseeing 12,000 cases that are complex, diverse and ever-changing. We are working with a computer program that lacks flexibility. It's hard for those in my office to respond to individuals requesting changes in support using the present system which is based only on past incomes, not on a father's desire to spend time with children."

Having (a) reassured the children's mother that you're not avoiding your responsibilities as the other parent, (b) placed relevant financial information in the court folder, and (c) filed the required forms at the courthouse and received the court's approval, you are more likely to be successful at achieving the following reasonable goals:

- Remain current with support payments
- Avoid wage attachments, job-search reports, and lectures from the judge
- Avoid paying the additional 10 percent interest penalty attached to child-support arrears
- Keep your driver's license and your assets in the checking account, and stay out of jail

Since lowering the number of hours that a father works can jeopardize both his relationship with his child's mother and his position at work, as a father you must ask yourself, "Is striving to spend more time with my children worth the risk?" It is, when the safety and comfort that a father's presence provides for his children outweighs the potential for conflict—then, of course, being available to the family is advisable. Don't worry. Remember that many single parents do change careers, every day. Changing careers may not be a viable option for you, but there is always some way to work out seeing your kids more often. Make sure to explore all options; it will be worth it to you and your kids.

Working Parents' Success Stories

More and more companies are accommodating single parents and realizing benefits from doing so. Owners, managers, and personnel departments are coming to see that they can count on these caring individuals. Divorced parents who are jointly responsible for their children are typically dependable, hard-working adults who are anchored by family to their communities. The same personality traits found in devoted parents (love and commitment) are benefits to companies. Many companies are willing to negotiate creative work schedules that allow for shared parenting.

Troy

Even many of the "macho" building trades are making room for moms and dads co-parenting their kids. Troy is a recently divorced, thirty-five-year-old contractor and also the father of two girls and a boy. His general contracting company employs thirty hard-working carpenters. A second-generation builder,

Troy, like his father, is trying to juggle raising his children with managing his company. "I understand how important it is for fathers to use up every minute of visitation time with their children. So, I allow the guys to leave the job early on Fridays and show up late on Monday if that is necessary to get their kids to school. I know visitation time is limited and that there is plenty of time in the week to make up for hours spent with kids."

Kyle

If you're a member of the unionized building trades (carpenter, electrician, etc.), you find yourself in the enviable position of being able to schedule time on and off the clock around your kids' visits when they live out of state. Kyle has been an electrician for thirteen years and divorced for three. "There was a lot of competition for jobs in Idaho," he says in explaining his reasons for moving to the Seattle area eighteen months ago. "I was struggling just to make ends meet and stay current on the child support. Katrina and I had a pretty good split, and we talked a lot about it before I moved. I also talked with Tyler (Kyle's ten-year-old son) quite a bit before I made the decision.

"Because I'm a master electrician, I get compensated pretty well here in Seattle," he says, because Seattle's building market is booming. "So I have the financial ability to fly Tyler out here every other weekend, and we talk on the phone all the time." What's more important though is that Kyle is really in charge of his own schedule in a lot of ways. "I can work as much or as little as I think I need to. I can double up during the weeks before one of Tyler's extended visits, like during summer and Christmas vacations, and not worry about the time off when he's here. Being able to maximize my face time with my son really helps us both get the most out of it. Tyler loves to hunt and fish, and that's something we do together, and when we're not together, we talk about hunting and fishing. It's not perfect, and I wish we were closer, but it's working pretty well, and with Tyler hitting those teen years, Katrina's going to need all the help she can get with him!"

Barrett

Barrett is a midlevel executive with a Silicon Valley technology firm. He moved to the West Coast from the Northeast two years ago. He has two kids: Jesse, eight, and Jenna, four. Where Kyle's job is classic blue collar, Barrett's is as white collar as they come. "I manage a team of fifteen," he says. "And you'd be amazed how much I can get done telecommuting in two to three days per week when the kids are here for short stays. I take vacation time for their longer vacations, because summer is our downtime anyway." What's more, Barrett points out that the conventional wisdom among many employers is shifting toward what many in the business call the "Microsoft" model when it comes to quality-of-life policies. "A happy employee is a more productive employee in the long run," he says. "I am very cognizant of that when entertaining requests for time off to do things with family, especially. So sharing custody of my kids has probably made me a more empathetic and more effective manager. Hey, like the man said, 'no one ever died thinking that they didn't spend enough time at work'!"

Co-Parenting Employees

It is becoming more commonplace for businesses to offer this type of nontraditional support to their co-parenting employees. It's no longer a big deal for single fathers to adjust their work schedules in order to fulfill their children's needs. With adequate planning, involved, co-parenting fathers are designing and implementing schedules that meet the needs of both their company and their family. When child care is blended into the work and parenting equation, long-distance parenting becomes that much easier for those who wish to parent more and work less.

Changing Your Work Schedule

Here is a checklist to refer to when drawing up a new, or refining an existing, work schedule:

1. How many hours can I work on parenting days?
   ❑ 4   ❑ 6   ❑ 8
2. Can I put in extra time on nonparenting days?
   ❑ 6   ❑ 8   ❑ 10
3. Is working four, or three, ten-hour days a possibility?
   ❑ yes   ❑ no   ❑ unsure
4. Can I work productively at home on parenting days?
   ❑ yes   ❑ no   ❑ unsure
5. Is my boss open to modifying my schedule?
   ❑ yes   ❑ no   ❑ unsure
6. Since I'm a long-distance divorced father, is my boss open to allowing me concentrated blocks of time off during the days when I have my children visiting me?
   ❑ yes   ❑ no   ❑ unsure
7. Will I be able to arrange child care for those days when I must work while my children are with me?
   ❑ yes   ❑ no   ❑ unsure
8. Does my parenting plan interfere with company goals?
   ❑ yes   ❑ no   ❑ unsure

9. Shown on a calendar, is my plan easily understandable?

   ❏ yes   ❏ no   ❏ unsure

10. Have I verbalized my proposed schedule to a friend?

    ❏ yes   ❏ no   ❏ not yet

11. Can I articulate my ideas concisely and confidently?

    ❏ yes   ❏ no   ❏ not yet

12. Am I willing to listen to and research alternative ideas?

    ❏ yes   ❏ no   ❏ unsure

13. If they say no, can I accept the rejection graciously?

    ❏ yes   ❏ no   ❏ unsure

Tips for Asking for a Modified Work Schedule

Armed with a well-thought-out plan, one that takes into account his responsibilities at work and allows for co-parenting, a father can now consider when, where, and to whom to make his request. When doing so, bear the following in mind:

- Timing is important: Talk with the boss when he can give you his full attention.
- Tailor the meeting to suit the management: Some managers prefer to discuss possible changes over business lunches. Others, especially those concerned with the employee's privacy, prefer to meet in the discreet environment of their own office. Suggest a setting where management is apt to feel relaxed enough to discuss *all* possible working schedules.
- Dress appropriately for your presentation: Do all you can to present yourself as an employee worth keeping.
- Make sure that you keep to the point; after all, this is about your kids.
- It is key for you to convince your boss that the company benefits from you getting blocks of time off when your kids are

in town. Talk about things like work-life balance and how a happy employee is a productive employee.

- Speak assertively: Explain what you have in mind, stress the benefits to the company with sincerity and conviction. Avoid emotional pleas. Remain professional.

Men, whether divorced or not, who survive the process of being separated from their family and move forward to create co-parenting arrangements can draw strength from having weathered some of life's most stressful challenges. As a result, such fathers can afford to feel confident. After all, they have the skills necessary to persuade an employer to accommodate long-distance parenting. Those who experience self-doubt may want to renew their spirits by remembering how far they have progressed since they became long-distance dads. Now for many dads, life has never been better, and more time with their children lies in the days ahead.

5

Building a
Support Network

SUPPORT. SAY IT WITH ME: "SUPPORT." LEARN it. Know it. Love it. It doesn't matter whether you're divorced and living away from your ex and your kids, whether you're a road warrior, whether you're deployed overseas or some combination of the above. Support is as integral a part of navigating the travails of being a long-distance dad as respect is. Not only financial and emotional support for your family and support for your ex (if you're divorced) when you're presenting a united parenting front, but support you yourself need. So let's talk about support networks!

Avoiding the Perception of Failure for Divorced Long-Distance Dads

Looking back to the day Nancy left with my daughter, I can still see myself standing dejectedly in the doorway of what used to be Stephany's house, blindly staring across our lawn and rosemary bushes. That had been our home, our slice of paradise. When my ex moved out and took our child, the emptiness in the home was devastating. My voice became the only one in the house, and my daughter's room grew more depressing with each load of toys that Nancy and Peter, her new boyfriend, hauled out. Fortunately, that time has passed, and today Nancy, Stephany, and I again enjoy positive lives.

Finding True Friends

It's during difficult times like these that you find out who your true friends are. And when it comes to value, friends like these are priceless. Sharing our sadness with others willing to help us with our burden can be such a blessing and such a relief! Those who care about us can validate our feelings by relating how they, too, have felt. That lessens our loneliness. Also, sharing with friends allows us to get insight into ourselves and our relationships with our exes.

My friend Tom is also a divorced father. He recalls telling his friend Mark, "I'm having the hardest time deciding if it would be better for my kids if they lived with their mother or if I should try for full custody."

The inability of Tom and his ex-wife to cooperate made a formal shared arrangement impossible. Just as I've already advised you to do, Tom went on to discuss his situation with friends. "Hearing men reassure me that I was going to be OK, parenting well, and doing a good job as a father was enabling," he says. "Being told you are doing well as a father is encouraging. It is always great to get support from other men."

A Disbanded Family Does Not Equal Failure

The idea that going through a family breakup means one is a failure is nonsense. One father confessed, "I was ashamed when my wife divorced me. All of a sudden, I was no better than all the others whose marriages had failed. My wife chose to leave and I'm a loser."

Here's how licensed marriage and family counselor Judith Goodman responded in an interview to sentiments such as those expressed above: "When we're triggered (re-feeling intensely), we need to remember that 90 percent of our feelings are from our past, and only the remaining 10 percent have anything to do with what is happening currently." During stressful times (like a divorce), fathers need to balance emotion with intellect. If you can remember that most of what you are feeling is being dredged up as a result of recalling events in the past, then reason can prevail and you've got a better chance to survive as a highly effective father. What's more, you won't have to entertain such commonplace fears as the one many fathers have, where they think that their children are not going to have good homes and receive the care and attention that these men long to provide.

As Goodman showed us above, sometimes we're dealing with something we can't lick on our own, and that is when it's a good idea for us to seek some sort of professional help.

Professional Help

Because counselors have emotional distance from the family, they can be both more objective regarding family issues and also less intimidating to children than their parents. Their being outside the family allows children the space to talk about issues that are too difficult, embarrassing, or frightening to share with Mom and Dad. And that can be a godsend for parent and child.

The counselor you hire can become a special friend to your child; this is good, but be cognizant of the need for limits.

Children need to know early on that the counselor's only purpose is to help them solve problems. Making sure the child understands that when the problems are solved, the visits will end is a good way to help your child keep the relationship in perspective. Without this understanding, children may come to believe that counselors are friends who will always be available for them.

A truly professional counselor will work hard to maintain the proper client-to-counselor boundary, thus preserving his or her own objectivity. He or she will keep in mind the financial cost to the parents and will not abuse the trust of either the child or the parents. Sit down with the counselor initially to set objectives for the counseling and observable outcomes to be achieved. Agree on a rough time frame for this to be accomplished. It's a good idea for parents to stay in the loop about what issues their children are working on, because a professional counselor can discuss that without blurring any confidentiality lines. Bear in mind, too, that if you develop any doubts about the professionalism of a counselor, it is absolutely appropriate for you to cease your child's visits with that counselor immediately.

Put Your Child's Needs First

My daughter has not seen or heard her parents argue in over ten years, and every week she witnesses two adults cooperating in order to provide for her. When Nancy and Peter bought a new home farther away from Stephany's school, Nancy chose to drive the extra twenty minutes, each way, so that her daughter could remain in the same school. She never suggested that Stephany and I change our lives to accommodate her choices. Mature choices like this one—placing the child's needs first and the parents' convenience second—are what help you build a climate of mutual respect and support.

Because her parents cooperate, Stephany also has the opportunity to observe two different lifestyles. Neither fits the *Leave It to Beaver* stereotype. In both homes the adults make sure that homework and chores are completed before it's time to play. At her mom's house, a ten-acre horse ranch, Stephany rides horses and takes care of dogs, cats, rabbits, chickens, and parrots. It's a busy place. Family vacations with her mom consist of camping trips to their mountain property and long rides through the Sierras. When she is at my house, our leisure time is spent socializing or traveling. Stephany will have friends over, or we'll visit them. During the summer, groups of us spend days at the beach. When she was two years old, we rode the train from California to Texas to visit her grandmother and granddad. There have been trips to Disneyland, Union Square, Candlestick Park, and Raging Waters. When she was nine, we explored Paris and Ireland, and when she was ten, we visited her brother, Gale, in Hawaii. Stephany was thirteen when we visited Australia and New Zealand. Exploring the theaters of London and Paris is next.

Other fathers who find that they can no longer cohabit with their children's mother agree that their children are better off with two homes. One reason they feel this way is that in a traditional family, there is always the opportunity for fathers to fall into the provider role and surrender the nurturing role to the mother. A long-distance father who has his children visit or stay with him has to cook dinner, do the laundry, make the bed, and read the bedtime story. By its very nature, the living situation gives fathers more opportunities to parent.

Make Time for Your Children
It is the father's responsibility to see to it that he has adequate time with his children, and cooperative parenting makes that

possible. Toni, a co-parenting mother, has noticed, "A lot of fathers become more involved when they are divorced . . . they're kind of forced into spending time with their kids. Because their partnership with the kid's mother did not work out, they have to look at what kind of relationship they want to have with their kids. If they want to be fathers, they have to do things they probably weren't doing before, like taking time off work to be with the kids. A lot of the time it was Mom who took on that role."

Think about it: if you're divorced, how many times did you make dinner or fix your kids a lunch before you and your spouse separated? How much laundry did you do? How often did you wipe your children's nose, change their diapers, take them to doctors' appointments, run them to school on your way to work, comfort them when they awoke in the middle of a nightmare?

Even if you were pretty good about splitting any and all of the duties listed above (and hundreds of others like them) with your ex, now that you're a long-distance parent who has more one-on-one time with your kids (as opposed to all of that two-parent time you had before), you're likely handling all of the little things a lot more now that you're on your own.

And that's a good thing. These little nurturing moments will help establish exactly the sort of routine that will help seal your bond with your kids. Sometimes building the foundation of a lifelong solid relationship with your kids really does come down to you being there to tie a shoe, kiss a scraped knee, run a bath, tell a bedtime story, or make a tuna-fish sandwich.

Shifting Your Priorities—Your Circle of Friends

Divorced long-distance dads may feel insecure when they begin spending more time with their children. It is a difficult transition to change their focus from work and money to kids and home economics. If your children's mother did most of the networking with other families, you may be without the company of other active parents. First and foremost, you've got to take steps to change that. Perhaps a church, synagogue, or mosque is the answer. If you already belong to one, you have no doubt figured out that worshipping in the manner you choose is hardly a solitary activity, and a place of worship of your choosing is a ready-made network for you to exploit. This is just one example, of course. There are others, such as fraternal organizations and volunteer work.

As your circle of friends expands, your loneliness should dissipate. Normally, it doesn't take fathers long to feel secure again. A man parenting with confidence is a pleasure to behold: ask any girl or boy laughing and wrestling with Dad in the park.

Dr. Tim Hartnett, himself a devoted father and a licensed marriage and family counselor, puts it this way: "The first decision Dad has to make is that his fathering is vital to the child, and counter the myth that mothers are more important to their children than fathers. Both mother and father have the same amount of humanness, and humanness is what's needed to parent children. A lot of men don't get in as much practice because of the way roles were divided before the divorce, so they feel more distant and less than adequate as parents."

When a father discovers that in order to feel good about himself he must continue as a parent, being restricted to visiting his child every other weekend becomes a humiliating and bitter experience. Often divorced men feel controlled by their ex-wives. In reality the culprit may be an antiquated family law system. (We will discuss this further in Appendix C, "Family Law.") After being restricted to *merely* visiting their children, many fathers feel manipulated, resentful, and cheated out of the opportunity to do what they love—spend time with their children. Criticism and suggestions from a man's ex-wife feel insulting. Paying child support often feels like salt in the wound, adding insult to injury.

By contrast, many fathers who are able to actively parent learn to trust their intuition. You can be a father who actively parents, even long-distance, and you can use technology (phone, e-mail, chat, etc.) to help you. (We'll address this more directly in the chapter on technology.) Marsha Sinetar, author of *Do What You Love, the Money Will Follow*, writes, "Turning our lives around is usually the beginning of maturity since it means correcting choices made unconsciously, without deliberation or thought." Such is the path of many men who realize they must be involved in the parenting of their children.

His church was a source of immense comfort for Greg R., a father whose contentious divorce left him bruised and bitter. Greg now facilitates divorce recovery groups in the church where he himself sought help. His advice:

"Open up, be vulnerable, let people know who you are, and what is going on. Five years ago, I told the people at the church's Divorce Recovery Group that it was difficult being a single father. They cared. Today, if a man wants to parent, help is available in most communities. Support and training have made a huge difference in my life."

Keith is the father of two girls, ages seven and two. He survived a divorce that was so violent he had to demand protection from the district attorney.

"I've learned a lot about myself, about my kids' needs and my past relationship with their mother. Today, I am only responsible for my kids, not their mother. I know what is important to me and what is not acceptable. Definitely I have grown in understanding and hopefully will continue to grow. It's been five years since my divorce, and looking back I've never felt more enlightened or empowered."

Currently, Keith cares for his children every other week.

New Organizations to Support Fatherhood

These days fathers around the country are showing how serious they are about shared parenting. Divorced dads, road warriors, and military fathers deployed overseas from all walks of life and every conceivable background, especially those practicing shared parenting, are beginning to help others to remain in their children's lives. As a result, societal attitudes about dads are changing. New organizations that support fatherhood are forming in cities across the United States. Groups built on the idea of peer support are being founded to assist the thousands of newly divorced fathers who find themselves and their families in crisis each year.

There may be such an organization in your local area. If not, there are sure to be single fathers eager to meet with men like themselves (a side-effect of the sad fact that divorce is so commonplace today). More and more, groups of dads are meeting regularly to discuss how to improve the condition of their families. At these friendly and informal gatherings, fathers are learning how to remain involved parents. Men are encouraged not to focus on what their ex-wives are doing; instead, fathers are learning the skills necessary to be the best of fathers, *no matter where they are*. In the company of such peers, men newly divorced get a reprieve from worry. Their imaginations are fired and life takes on greater meaning. For an hour each week they can sit among friends and enjoy a fellowship built around a noble cause—sustaining the well-being of each other's families. No longer must a man sit alone and ponder what to do about child custody. Today, at the very least, there is peer support through the Internet; the URL *www.divorcedfathersnetwork.org* will take you to a Web site where you can find support.

How to Start a Divorced Fathers Network

Those who live in communities where meetings do not exist may want to start groups of their own. The first thing needed is a text. My first book, *Fathers Are Forever: A Co-Parenting Guide for the Twenty-First Century*, is often used for the teaching of shared parenting. In a group setting, the information within its chapters can be used for topics of discussion. Mothers and fathers can limit their exposure to conflict by following the suggestions printed on these pages. Because shared parenting is a long process and opportunities for misunderstandings do occur during the years it takes to raise children, most parents choose to keep *Fathers Are Forever* for future reference.

When starting a group, it is helpful to have a copy of my booklet, *Starting a Divorced Fathers Network*. It can be purchased on the Internet at *www.divorcedfathers.com*. The booklet explains how to run the meetings, network within one's community, and sustain the group as it grows.

There are tremendous benefits to reaching out to the fathers in your community. When I was struggling in the early days of my family's breakup, a wise gentleman suggested to me that I stood to gain more from speaking with men going through divorce than I possibly could from relying on people like himself, far removed from the resources and process of divorce. His words rang true. I believe his advice saved my relationship with my daughter and possibly even my life. A fellow named Tom was the first divorced father I spoke with, twenty years ago. He, too, was alone and suffering through visits with his children one afternoon a week. Tom understood completely how painful it was for me to be separated from my daughter. I looked forward to our meetings and always felt better after our conversations. We compared the gains and losses we experienced in our quests to create shared parenting. I owe much of my success as a father to the fathers who have talked with me.

For the past twenty years Nancy and I have cooperatively raised Stephany. Today, our lives are far removed from the nightmarish days when she and I first parted ways. Stephany was a toddler then; today, she is twenty-two—as healthy an individual as one will ever meet. After years of shared experiences, both painful and joyous, my relationship with Nancy can best be described as a blend of respect and friendship. For us the drama of the past is inconsequential. To date, we have raised a healthy child. Still, there are pressing issues to contend with. It is a big job to fulfill the needs of a young adult, especially when she is juggling family and friends. Nancy and Stephany still ride horses. My daughter and I recently returned from one extended vacation and are planning our next one.

I have committed myself to the purpose of helping divorced fathers fulfill their need to parent. As a result, each week I enjoy the company of men who, like myself, feel there is nothing more important than their role as a father. New dads attending our gatherings find a fellowship of men sharing laughter and compassion. Our meetings are inspiring; we know that the work we do benefits those involved. Lives are saved, relationships are altered for the better, and harmony is restored to families. Dads become well versed in shared parenting, and some in time move on and become leaders, founding groups in other cities, thus the network of fathers and the idea of shared parenting grows. There are few relationships that mean more to me than the ones I form with devoted dads.

To ensure that tomorrow's dads have every chance to raise their own children, today's fathers need to pass on to them the skills necessary to co-parent. Self-control during trying times, proficiency in learning parenting and communication skills, and unwavering commitment to their children—these are the traits successful long-distance parents model. By our actions we can guarantee that the next generation of fathers will have every opportunity to nurture their children.

Finding Support for Deployed Dads

While you're serving abroad, there are resources available to you if you are looking for support. There are other men who are also missing their children and dealing with trying to be fathers from afar. Chaplains and other religious officials are available to talk to and lean on as a source of support. There is also access to psychologists if you feel the need to talk to someone in that capacity.

Once you return, the VFW is a great resource for dads who are having trouble getting used to being back with their children or who just need a little support in general. Here, you will find support groups for every group of fathers that has served in the military. It's also a place to find support from other men and women who have been in the military and shared experiences similar to yours. Try to maintain connections with the men and women that you served with and talk to others going through the same thing. Counseling can also help soldiers readjust to being back with their kids. This is always a good resource. Contact the Department of Veterans Affairs at *www.va.gov* for more information.

Finding Support for Road-Warrior Dads

For many fathers on the road, life is a lonely business. Sleeping alone, restaurants filled with strangers, menus that list the same fare, motel rooms that bed a parade of tired long-distance dads; these are the obstacles that must be overcome before the opportunity to savor the evening phone call back home. What have the kids done today? How is the wife—part-time single mom—holding up? Now is the long-distance dad's chance to tell someone who loves him exactly how relieved he is to be able to tell those he loves how his day has gone. The evening phone call can often feel like a life preserver in the sea of humanity to the father on the road. Use your family as a support system from afar if at all possible.

If you need support in a way that your family cannot provide, at least from a distance, churches have support groups of varying types and activities almost every night. No matter where you are, you can find these by looking online or in a phone book. This works even better if you know ahead of time where you will be. No matter where you are, you can also find community-based resources for opportunities to socialize and be with other people, which can be a blessing when traveling alone.

6

Children Newborn to Age Five

WOW, TALK ABOUT A TOUGH ROW TO HOE. FOR whatever reason, you find yourself the absentee father of a very, very small child. This begs the question: How are you, as the child's father, supposed to bond with your little one if you're either not the custodial parent or away from home because of work all the time?

Don't despair, there are ways around this problem! First, we'll take a look at some of the basic characteristics of a child in this age range, both at their behavior and what their specific needs are. Although there is no question that you have a challenge ahead of you, don't forget that in many languages, concepts such as "challenge" and "opportunity" are represented by the same word. So make the most of your opportunity.

Newborn to Age Five: Characteristics and Specific Needs

It is no secret that children grow and change more over their first five years than over the rest of their childhood combined. Children this age are incredibly dependent on their parents and/or care providers for having their material needs (food, clothing, shelter, etc.) met.

Children this age also imprint on those around them when they are young and tend to build bonds that, when nurtured properly, will last their entire lives. Children at this age learn to share and to play well with others, and they attach themselves emotionally to those who teach them how to do these things, for good or ill.

They learn to communicate both verbally and nonverbally, they learn to walk, they become self-aware, they begin to make sense of the world around them as something other than a jumble of sensory input. And you're missing a large part of it. Yikes!

Children of this age are starting to need more strict boundaries. In his book *Father and Child Reunion: How to Bring the Dads We Need to the Children We Love*, Warren Farrell says, "How does treating boundaries seriously create empathy? Teaching the child to treat boundaries seriously teaches the child to respect the rights and needs of others. Thinking of another's needs creates empathy. A child who learns that consequences are always negotiable focuses on how to manipulate the best negotiation, or on its desires, not the desires and needs of the person setting the boundary—or the person who is being intruded upon when the boundary was violated. I remember hearing when I was a kid, 'good fences make good neighbors,' without understanding the deeper reasons why."

Marriage and family counselor (and father) Tim Hartnett thinks that it's never too early to start building your relationship with your child, especially if that child is a daughter. The father-daughter dynamic is important on many levels and begins very early on. He says, "If a child comes from a family where there is bitterness from divorce, the mother may have negative attitudes about men in general and Dad in particular. The father needs to be present to show his daughter exactly who he is. When girls have a strong sense that men will love them for reasons other than their sexuality—and that is what their dads can provide—then girls stand a better chance of avoiding dysfunctional, oversexualized relationships. If Dad says, 'I love you because you are my daughter, because of who you are,' when his girl is approached by a guy who only wants sex, she may pass the guy by and keep looking for what she knows is possible—a man who loves her for who she is."

But it's not just the daughters who need Dad's positive presence in their lives from birth onward. For young children of both genders, *who* you are as their father is nearly as important as what you do for them directly.

What You Can Do for Your Newborn to Five-Year-Old from Afar

Assuming that you have the assistance of your child's mother, you have a lot of options open to you for keeping yourself involved in your young child's life (if not, see Chapter 12). Here are some ways that you can keep yourself in the mix:

Pictures, Pictures, Pictures!

The more your child sees of you, the more he or she is able to imprint on you. So make sure that there are plenty of pictures of yourself in your child's room. You can do this in a variety of ways: Make a photo album of you and your child doing things together, and when you have time with each other, sit down with your child and look at the pictures. You can also do such things as having photos of yourself laminated and made into things like bookmarks and placemats. You can even have your picture printed on a pillowcase!

Dad Door

The back side of the door to your child's room is a terrific place to set up a visual display that helps reinforce your child's bond to you: make it into a "Dad Door," and put up pictures of you and your child doing things you love to do together (fishing, baseball, playing chess, scrapbooking, what have you) there. Also put a map of the state/country/world on your Dad Door, with arrows pointing to where your child lives and to where you are that week/month/year. There are all sorts of things you can do with this one. Run with it; have fun with it!

Sounds

Do you remember when you were a child, and perhaps one of your parents (or a grandparent?) would tuck you in and either tell you a story or read to you until you dropped off to sleep? If you didn't have this as a child, it's probably something for which you justifiably longed. This is something else that is easy to do to keep your child imprinting on you and recognizing your voice. Take some time to record yourself reading a favorite bedtime story in a soothing, affectionate tone. Even newborns can be lulled merely by the sound of your voice, and this doesn't have to be played just at bedtime; it can be played whenever your toddler is settling down for all-too-infrequent quiet time, and mom needs a break.

In fact, if you've got the technology (see our chapter on technology), there's nothing to say that you can't record a video of yourself reading to your child, and it can be watched either on the computer monitor or on the television, in lieu of something like *Blues Clues* or *Dora the Explorer.* But don't just stop there. Get your child a speakerphone and you can be there to "virtually" tuck him or her in from time to time. Also, if you can get your child a speakerphone with speed dial as a function of the phone, once your child is learning to use the phone (obviously this will take place closer to age five than to the day your child was born), you can program your own telephone number into his or her phone, and your child will know that he or she can talk to you anytime he or she wants to or needs to. This reassurance can be of enormous comfort to your child.

Smell

If you have a favorite cologne, something that your child can easily identify with you, perhaps you can spray it on a sweater, T-shirt, or sweatshirt (I got this idea from Mr. Rogers) and hang it in your child's closet, then when you "get home," you can put this sweater on, and the child further identifies it with you.

Birthdays

If your child spends his or her birthday (I'm thinking of months with no vacation time in them) away from you every year, there are ways to still keep yourself in the loop on his or her big day. When your child is young like this, try "money cards," where you give him or her a card a day for every year of their age preceding their birthday; for example, five cards per day during the five days that lead up to their fifth birthday, and in each card, put one dollar (this can get expensive as they get older!). A dad named Paul gave his son a brass compass one year, with the inscription on it, "May you always find your way home." His son still treasures that compass.

Here are some ideas for special birthday presents you can give to your young child:

- A video of dad, reading a bedtime story and saying I love you and always will.
- A custom shirt and sipping cup with a picture of Dad and the child doing something they enjoy together are items the child can use daily and have as regular reminders of his or her long-distance dad.
- Have a book made and put the child's name, the father's name, and the mother's name in the book.

Obviously, with this age group you are constrained with regard to what you can do to have a daily role in your child's life, but these suggestions are easy to do, feasible to implement, and can have a powerful impact on your child's bonding with you.

Three Problems Facing Dads with Newborns to Five-Year-Olds

The three most common problems that long-distance fathers of children this age can anticipate are:

- Father's feeling of loss of contact with his kids.
- Depression arising from the struggle to accept a frequently awkward new living situation.
- Concerns about how to handle emergencies that may occur when they're away from their children.

These are understandable concerns, and as such they are serious and deserving of consideration. There are simple (note that I didn't say "easy") solutions that can help you mitigate the effects of these all-too-common problems. So let's talk solutions!

Three Solutions

Here are some brief solutions to the problems outlined above. More in-depth answers follow.

- Suggest to your children's mother that you take the kids for a few days in order to give her time to visit family, take a vacation, or have some time to herself.
- Join a club, volunteer, or become a mentor. Getting involved in your community can help take your mind off of the fact that your children are not there with you. If you're feeling sad in a way that activities cannot help with, seek the advice of a counselor.
- Make sure to plan ahead and talk to your children's mother about what might happen if an emergency were to occur while the kids are with her or with you. Have this plan written down so that you are both prepared.

Making More Time with Your Kids

First, feeling that you're losing contact with your kids can really get you down if you let it. Here's a potential solution: the next time you're bemoaning the loss of quality time with your young one, try looking at some of the challenges your child's mother is taking on. In many ways, her situation is the exact reverse of your own: where you don't get enough time with your kid, she likely doesn't get enough time to herself.

It is entirely possible that this will afford you more than an altered perspective. It is possible that if approached respectfully and in a mature fashion, Mom's need of a break every once in a while can help you ensure that you get more time with your kids. Regardless of outcome, it's something to think about. For instance, you might suggest that you could watch the kids while she goes to visit her parents, spends a day at a spa, or takes a weekend vacation. Be sensitive to your wife or ex-wife's feelings; if she is not receptive to the idea of giving you the kids in this manner, do not push her.

Depression Stemming from Time Away from Your Kids

Next, there is the question of how to deal with the depression that arises from learning to accept a new living situation that doesn't include your kids. Here are some possible solutions:

- Spend time with people who understand what you are going through. Look around you—there are dads like yourself in your neighborhood, at work, and at the gym. No matter what your interests, there will be another father involved who knows exactly what it is like to be without his kids. Talk about what is going on in your life, be sure and listen to his experiences, and don't offer advice unless it is asked for. Brainstorm with dads like yourself and you are almost certain to hear some new ideas that might raise your spirits.

- Volunteer in your community. Don't forget that it feels good to help others. When some people feel depressed and are focusing only on themselves, they escape their self-centeredness by assisting others.

- Counseling is always an option. Most people spend more on their car's maintenance then they invest in their own peace of mind. If the budget is tight, join a men's group, facilitated or not. If you can afford it and prefer a marriage and family counselor, hire one. Why not look for one who uses a sliding scale (the amount you pay is adjusted based on your income) in his or her billing? Invest in yourself.

■ Invest in yourself for a few reasons: (a) You matter; you are as important as any other person; (b) Your kids need a healthy dad; (c) You can model for your kids how one takes care of him- or herself during challenging times.

Dad to Dad

This isn't some Woody Allen movie, and I'm no Hollywood actor going on and on about how close I am to my analyst. But I'm here to tell you: divorce, isolation, and adjusting to having your kids around less can be incredibly traumatic—the psychic equivalent of a heart attack. Would you leave a heart attack untreated and try to just "tough it out"? Only if you're crazy.

Why then would you forego an opportunity to get perspective, to address those feelings that can drive you to despair? In this society, men are expected to ignore or suppress their feelings. Here's something that is common knowledge among therapists and family counselors alike, though: if you repress your feelings and don't address how they can affect your daily life—from your work performance to your stress levels to your parenting abilities— they will manifest themselves in other, unhealthy ways.

So, finding an outlet for these negative feelings is really an important part of being an effective long-distance father at this stage of your child's life: whether it be exercise, talking with other divorced fathers, attending church or other social groups, or some combination of the above, an outlet is everything in this situation.

Next time you're getting down on yourself because of your living situation, try repeating this series of affirmations. Since it's natural to feel initially overwhelmed by divorce/separation, among other things, you might find yourself repeating these affirmations almost hourly. Eventually, as you progress in your understanding and acceptance of your situation, hopefully they will become no more than a daily routine. Here they are:

- My children are a gift and no one has the right to stand between them and me.
- I am a capable parent and I enjoy being with my children.
- I teach my kids what I know and am there for them when they need me.
- The time I spend with my children benefits them more than the money I earn working.

And for feelings that can't be dealt with by exercise, talking to other dads, or daily affirmations, there is health care available out there. Once you get past the stigma of how it might make you look with your poker buddies, it's in your best interest to make sure that you are healthy, both mentally and physically, for the sake of those who are so completely dependent upon you.

Time Spent with Your Child at Your Child's Home

For fathers still married to their children's mother (road warriors and deployed dads), when you're home, you've really got to make the most of the time available to you where your kids are concerned. This goes double for divorced dads who are visiting their children from outside the area (after all, your child has a life at home with his or her mom, family, and friends, and it's mostly independent of the life he or she shares with you when the two of you are at your place).

How to make the most of visits with your children in their hometown? Enjoy yourself and explore your children's world. Even if you are familiar with the area, view yourself as a visitor to their town; there is a lot for you to learn, and children love showing their parents all the places they like to go and the things they like to do. Be the chauffer, take care of the travel arrangements, and let your child be the guide. No matter where your children are, there will be hundreds of things they would love to share with you. All but the youngest children will be able to show you the things that interest them.

If your child is too young to talk, put him or her in a backpack and go exploring. It is delightful to walk around your children's neighborhood with your child peering over your shoulder. If you run into the neighbors, take a moment and introduce yourself. Get to know those who see your child daily. Let them know something about you. Keep it positive—sure you're a long-distance dad and they may see your child more often than you do, but they are not your child's father and that puts you in a class all your own.

If the children are old enough to talk, ask for a tour of their room. Explore every nook and cranny of the closet, toy chest, and library. If your children have a favorite book, take time to read it. Really get into it. Sit on the floor so that you are close to the same height as they are, relax, and read. Make an effort to see their world as they see it. It is fun for parent and child.

Ask about their favorite play areas. If they mention the park, ask them to show you around. Take a tour with your favorite tour guide. Where in the park do they like to play—swings, monkey bars, sandbox, basketball court, skateboard park, bike trails? Educate yourself on exactly what they like most about the location. How does it make them feel—free, wild, crazy, brave, happy? They will love to tell you all about it, especially if you are sincerely interested and enjoy hearing them explain themselves. Be sure and play with them at their favorite game, but be careful to remember your age and limitations—too many well-intentioned dads have hurt themselves trying to keep up with their kids. If you don't know how to skateboard in the half-pipe, don't try it yourself, just watch your kids and cheer them on.

Also, when your child is doing something important, something special to them (acting in a play, performing in a music recital, getting a merit badge in a ceremony at a Scouting meeting, anything along these lines), something where they will be recognized publicly for their achievement, if you can possibly manage it, *be there.* Take the time off work, make the travel arrangements, don't miss this opportunity to be not only a part of your child's life at this most auspicious of moments, but also to be part of the cherished memories of times like this. There is very little you can do that will more forcefully and visibly demonstrate the strength of your commitment and the depth of your devotion to your children.

Because of the 483,514 children of active-duty military members and 177,888 children of reserve and Guard members under the age of five, Sesame Workshop and Wal-Mart have joined forces to launch a new program called *Talk, Listen, Connect: Helping Families During Military Deployment.* Through the program, free kits are being made available via the Department of Defense through Military OneSource. For more information on the bilingual program, visit *www.sesameworkshop.org/tlc.*

Daily Care

Many long-distance fathers find themselves constantly fretting about the "what-ifs" of daily life. What will happen if their child needs emergency care? What happens to their children if something happens to them? How will they be provided for?

It's understandable that a long-distance father would be concerned about these issues, because acknowledging that these sorts of things happen in everyday life is also acknowledgment of a loss of a certain amount of control over that aspect of your life for which you likely feel most responsible: the care of your children. So what can you do about it?

- Have a plan.
- Make sure your affairs are in order.
- Make a living will. This is easy to do; simply do an online search for "living will" and you'll be presented with several downloadable options. Fill it out, have it notarized, and you're all set.

Think about it: you know who your kids' doctor is, right? Why not sit down with your kids' mother and lay out an emergency plan involving who their doctor is, what hospital is the preferred one in case of emergency, insurance info, and so on. Once you've got that all written out, copy it, and keep at least two copies in every place where your kids will spend time (relatives such as grandparents, your own place, your vacation home/cabin if you have one, etc.). If your kids will be visiting you in your "long-distance" home, talk it over with their mother and have a plan for what will happen if they get sick while with you. Show her that you're responsible by checking out local doctors' offices and hospitals before having this conversation.

Then there's the question of how to best ensure your kids will be taken care of in case something terrible happens to you. Do your children a favor. Years before your last day, create a living trust. Then you know that your final wishes will be honored and your children stand to inherent your wealth without struggle. It can be emotionally challenging to address death and settle final issues pertaining to money, your wife, and your children. Yet there is a sense of satisfaction when your house is in order.

More to the point, it's taking the broad and proactive steps of actively working to control those things that are in your purview to control, and not bothering with that which lies beyond the pale of your ability to bother even trying to control it.

Not much, you say? Well, it's a start, and like the man said, "Rome wasn't built in a day."

7

Children Ages Six to Ten

"I live in Maine and my dad lives in Chicago. My folks have been divorced since I was two, but I can't remember a time when I needed him that my dad wasn't there. I remember how he surprised me the weekend before my first day of first grade by flying out from Chicago and spending the weekend with me. We went to dinner and to the park, and he took me to the movies, too. Then, on my first day of school, Dad walked me to school to make sure I knew the way. I couldn't ask for a better dad."—Ryanne, now age fifteen

WHILE THE LEARNING CURVE FOR KIDS AGES six through ten isn't nearly as high as it is for newborns through five-year-olds, there is no question that they still develop at an incredible rate and are beginning to figure out the way the world works, as opposed to just existing in it. This chapter will deal directly with how to cope with your child's growing awareness of the uniqueness of your family's situation, and what you can do to ensure that they do so in a positive manner. We will discuss everything from counseling to the ongoing endeavor to ensure the best possible maintenance of the family's routine.

Child Counseling

We've dealt with the importance of counseling for adults in previous chapters, but now we'll address the importance of counseling for your children. After all, being separated from your immediate family is tough enough on adults, who are (at least in theory) emotionally equipped to deal with any sort of massive, potentially traumatic life change. Who wouldn't want their child to have an extra leg up in their own struggle to make sense of a world that they're still only barely coming to understand?

Also, for parents who are honestly committed to their children, a counselor can be an incredible resource in ensuring that the lines of communication between both parents and their kids remain open, established, and fully functioning.

If you think your child is having a problem dealing with your being away, talk to the counselor at your child's school. You can tell if your child is having a problem with your absence by talking to him or her and hearing him or her voice fears. For example, if your child hears about a plane crash on the news and knows that you have to fly often for business, your child could internalize the news story and fear for your safety. It could be worth it to have your child talk to a counselor who is an expert on children and how they rationalize thoughts. This is also helpful for children of parents going through divorce, which is often the biggest life-changing event in a child's life.

You Can't Fool Your Kids, So Don't Bother to Try

Children in general are very aware of what goes on around them. Kids aged six to ten are such information sponges that they tend to miss even less. And it's during this age period that they tend to start putting together how the world works (a divination process that becomes even more refined during their second decade of life, and a topic that we will revisit in Chapters 8 and 9).

Julio, a road-warrior dad from Phoenix, Arizona, discovered this one day when he came home from his truck-driving job and had the chance to drive his daughter home from school. "One day Corina and I were walking to my car and we were talking about her day at school and she told me that her friend, Samantha, had been talking about how much she was going to miss her daddy when he went away just like Corina misses me when I am gone. I was sad until Corina told me that when Samantha said that, Corina gave her a hug and then she told Samantha to ask her father to get her a counselor to talk to. Samantha's dad is in the National Guard and is probably going to war, and Corina recognized that Samantha was afraid. The idea to use a counselor is one of the things I taught her. The acceptance of my work schedule and being away nine days for every two home is something her counselor helped her with."

If your child is aware that you're hurting, at this stage of their development, they're probably going to feel responsible for it. This is true whether you're going through a divorce or just sad about being away from the family for some time. Marriage and family counselor Claudia Alonzo puts it this way:

"Kids always know how their parents feel, but unfortunately, in knowing everything, they also, because of how kids think, assume they caused it—they made the situation or feeling happen. I think it just goes with the way a child (at this age) looks at the world and the universe—they're the center of the universe—that's how children think. That's developmentally what children ought to be thinking when they're little. When parents are having a difficult time, their kids often jump to the conclusion that they caused the problem."

Gary is a road warrior who spends about half of each month out of town visiting clients. He and his wife, Marilyn, have two daughters: Michele, age eight, and Michaela, age six. Gary remembers one time when he got unexpectedly called out of town right before a family reunion barbecue. Unsure whether he would make it back in time for the big event, he pretended as if he was certain that he would, and his very young daughter called him on it. "'Daddy,' Michele said to me, 'Are you OK? You seem sad. What's wrong?' Poor thing thought someone had died, the way I was moping and saying everything was just fine. I had to laugh or I'd have started to cry," he recalls. "So I told her the truth, that I was disappointed that I had to leave so close to the barbecue, and that I wasn't sure if I'd make it back to town in time to go. 'That's OK, Daddy,' she said. 'We'll save you 'tato salad!' Michele thinks everyone loves potato salad as much as she does. My wife and I still laugh about that every summer when reunion time rolls around again."

Not only are we wasting our time when we lie to kids, but by not assuming responsibility for our actions, we allow children to take on guilt that is not theirs.

In the long run, we protect our children by being honest about our feelings—so long as we're careful not to burden them with our emotions. Children need to be excluded from their parents' drama as much as possible. However, it is admittedly a fine line for a parent to walk. On the other hand, kids don't miss much at this age, and anyone who's parented a six- to ten-year-old will tell you that they're usually not shy about asking questions!

Don't Be Afraid to Show Emotion

Counselors will tell you that children ask difficult questions only when they feel safe. Most of the fathers I work with are not afraid to show their emotions to their children—they believe it is healthy to do so—and most know how important it is to maintain self-control. This means as fathers we may cry, but we don't emotionally fall apart. Some children feel insecure when their parents are sad, and when that happens, fathers simply remind them that dads take care of kids even when they are sad.

Children are tuned in to their parents. When their mom or dad is upset, it upsets them. This is a survival tool established hundreds of generations ago when children paid attention to their parents as a way to avoid danger. Today, of course, avoiding danger is not the same as it was back in the days of the hunter-gatherers. Instead, there are other perilous situations, such as fathers going off to war and families experiencing divorce and separation.

It is the long-distance dad's job to reassure his children that he will remain in their lives. This can be difficult if Dad is feeling sad about leaving his children, or anxious about a journey he must take. Spend a half hour with your child, reassuring her or him through your manner that you are capable of taking care of the job ahead and that there is not a moment in a day that you do not love him or her, and that you are committed to being his or her father forever.

For Jonathan, a merchant marine living in San Jose, his talk with his kids looks like this: He explains his agenda over a snack of peanut butter on crackers and small glasses of Pepsi. "I'm leaving for Seattle way early tomorrow morning, so I won't see you off to school." There is a clamor of whining little voices, and despite the fact that he also feels saddened by his departure, he puts on a brave face and says, "I have to go and whining won't make it easier. So let's not go there. It is up to me to captain the boats and that's what I do to make the money we need to enjoy such a good life. Make sense? Now I'd rather hang out with you two any day of the week, but that is not what is going to happen." He ends the conversation with, "Do you two know I love you? I'll miss you both and I count the days until I'm home aground. Thirty-two days this time."

It's also important to validate your children in symbolic ways. This can be instructive as well as emotionally affirming, because we as parents never stop being role models for our children. Listening and talking with them, giving hugs or verbal validation, and telling our children we love them—daily—does more to make them feel secure than anything else we might do, and it also shows them appropriate ways to show affection. Gifts bought are quickly forgotten, but intimate moments shared by a father and his child can last a lifetime.

The point is that kids need to know their fathers love them and will always be there. Who wants to be the father of the child who, now grown, can't remember ever hearing Dad say "I love you"?

Children Age Six to Ten: Characteristics and Specific Needs

Children of this age need a sense that their father is there for them and that as kids they are not alone. They need to be aware of their father's presence even if he is not with them full-time. Long-distance dads can still provide a sense of "I am here" for their kids when they are away. It is an awareness that the child carries, the feeling of "I need not worry, I have a dad."

Divorced dads establish their presence by giving their children the message that they are not going to abandon them despite the fact that they will not be living together full-time. Road-warrior dads establish their presence by letting their children know the destination where they can be found and when they will return. It is the father's job to maintain his presence by providing his destination and letting his children know if there is a change in plans so they can reach their father whenever they need to. Military and deployed dads establish and maintain their presence by providing a means to stay in contact with their children. Their children need the most reliable e-mail address or mailing address so they know that their words will reach their fathers.

Children ages six to ten also need to know that, to their father, who they are matters. Fathers need to affirm that in practical ways, with words and actions. Long-distance dads can let their children know they matter by saying, "I know who you are and I value you." The fact that a father knows who his child is and will love him or her unconditionally affirms the child.

A strong characteristic of girls at age ten and boys a year or two later is that they begin to look at the world from a more adult perspective and strongly tend to put themselves in adult roles with adult responsibilities. This is particularly prone to happen when Dad is not in the home. So, parents in these situations will have to carefully manage this, allowing children to take adult roles and responsibilities when it serves the child's development and confidence, but be very careful about children taking on more adult responsibilities than they have the tools and maturity to handle. Unfortunately, it can be convenient and easy for Mom and Dad to allow this happen. In the boy–mom situation, the boy becomes the man of the house (he might even *mistakenly* be told this). In the girl–dad situation, it can be tempting for the ten-year-old girl to start being the little domestic who washes the dishes, prepares simple meals, and does housework.

Three Problems Facing Long-Distance Fathers of Six- to Ten-Year-Olds

Here are three common problems that parents of six- to ten-year-olds face:

1. The child taking on the role of caretaker. Tom noticed that when Claire, his seven-year-old, spent time with him, she tried to take care of him. "At first it was just odd, then I became concerned because she began to act more like a parent than a child."
2. Children don't enjoy spending time with Dad when he is home because he is the disciplinarian.
3. Children of this age are sometimes afraid to disappoint their parents. Almost every child experiences the feeling of being afraid to disappoint his or her parents. A little of this fear is natural. But children who are overly afraid are apt to be unhappy.

Three Solutions

Here are solutions to the problems outlined above:

1. If children hear, from their mothers, "Your dad will be home soon. He's probably going to be tired from jet

lag, so I want you to be considerate of his feelings, don't make a bunch of noise, he is only home for a couple of days, so be good," they could turn that comment into the feeling that their father is flawed and needs to be cared for. Children ages six to ten are self-focused, so it is unnatural for them to be providers or protectors of their parents. It is very unnatural for a child to try and comfort her father, especially when she or he is supposed to be excited to see him. If this situation arises, it is the father's role to reassure his children that as their father, he is entirely capable of taking care of both his needs and theirs. A lighthearted explanation of roles is a good idea: "Claire, I traveled halfway around the world to see my favorite little girl, so how about this: you be the little girl you are and I'll be the daddy I am? Now let's go for a bike ride."

2. This family dynamic is as troubling for long-distance dads as it is for their children. No father wants to return home only to hear stories of how his child misbehaved and have the task laid at his feet of "making his kid tow the line." No one should be viewed only as the enforcer of the family. Mothers and fathers need to share that task, especially when the kids are in the six-to-ten age range, so that one parent does not appear as the constant disciplinarian and kids feel that they can get away with something when that person is not around.

3. Billy, an eight-year-old, knew that his dad would be mad about his getting detention after school for talking in class. Because he feared his father's disappointment, Billy forged his dad's name on the detention slip he was supposed to show his parents. Poor Billy's plan failed

and he was caught when his parents arrived at the regular time to pick him up and he was not at the curb, but was in the classroom serving his time. Nice try, Billy. A child's fear of disappointing his or her father can be assuaged by a father who remembers to ask every so often, "Do you know that I love you and that I always will?" When the children answer yes, Dad's house is in order.

Child Care

There are numerous forms of child care available for children of every age. The means of supervision range from hiring a nanny to forming a cooperative babysitting network where you and other parents take turns looking after one another's kids. When a father makes up his mind as to what he feels will work best for his child, he can start looking for the appropriate child care.

What do you do if you live in a new place where you don't know the neighbors, let alone who the good babysitters are, and you know you're going to have your kids for a week soon and won't be able to get off work for the entire week?

The most important thing to do (and stop me if you've heard this before) is to have a plan. Many churches provide day camps, as do YMCA chapters, and these can be great experiences for kids who live out of the area most of the year. These are just two options. There are a plethora of others out there.

Some fathers mistakenly feel that the time their children spend at child care is not productive. Supervised peer playtime at an age-appropriate facility is developmentally critical for children ages six through ten. What's more, it gives parents a break! Let's face it, the playtime that your kids spend with friends doesn't just free you and your kids' mother up to make a living and provide for your families; the *downtime* that your kids' playtime affords you will help make you a much better parent in the long run!

Private Child Care

When children are too young to attend kindergarten and fathers need time to work, private child care can be a solution. There are various types of institutions ranging from commercial businesses located in shopping malls to licensed individuals who supervise four or five children in the privacy of their own homes. State-licensed day care is preferable, although a license does not necessarily guarantee good child care. Licensing does require that basic standards be met and, of course, it is always appropriate for parents to ask to see the child-care provider's license.

Sharing Child Care with Other Parents

Cooperative parenting worked well for me. Parenting every other week and rotating child care with other parents means watching kids one or two working days every other week. My daughter was able to play with her friends and I was able to meet my work obligations. I would either take the girls with me or work at home. Adjusting my work schedule to allow for the supervision of three children for two days every other week was manageable.

When I had to work and could not personally provide child care, I would hire a babysitter who met the preapproved qualifications that Cathy, Annette, and I had initially set. Generally we hired a teenager who had been recommended by our circle of friends. When outside help was required, we always sought the approval of our other parents in advance. Since we were all from the same community, we never had to hire a stranger.

A reminder: when laying out this schedule, listen to your children's input. If they happen to tell you they don't like a particular babysitter or a child-care facility, ask them why. Your kids may be telling you that there is poor supervision, or even abuse occurring.

Shared Child Care Success from One Long-Distance Dad

Dave is a tech-industry guy divorced from his ex-wife, Johnna, for five years. His son Mike is eight, and Dave gets Mike during most school holidays, including two months during summer vacation. Dave is a contractor and can work as much or as little as he likes in short bursts, but he can't afford to take off the entire summer to spend with Mike. So while he takes time off to be with Mike during the other school breaks, Dave makes the most of summer vacation by pooling his resources with his cousin Karen, a third-grade teacher, and her neighbor Trina, an attorney.

"This works great," Dave says. "All three kids get along well *most of the time*, they're roughly the same age, and during the summer, we alternate weeks. I take them one week, then work the next two, Karen takes them the second one, and Trina the third, then we start over. This way I don't take too much of a hit financially by having Mike here, and we don't get sick of each other because we're together every waking minute of the day.

"On top of that, each of us parents takes the kids on some sort of different outing while we have them on any given week. Mike and I both love to hike, so we'll do that a couple of

CHILDREN AGES SIX TO TEN

different days during my weeks; Trina loves to shop, so they go downtown a couple of days a week, and Karen has a thing for museums and boat rides, so it's a nice mix. It's not always perfect, working within our combined schedules and around the odd crabby day each kid may be having, but all in all, it's working pretty well."

Getting to Know the Parents of Your Child's Friends

"It takes a village to raise a child" is an African saying made popular in the United States by Senator Hillary Clinton. The phrase carries a message that can make a world of difference for dads. Divorced fathers who must move out of their old neighborhood can still help their children and themselves adjust to the move by initiating friendships with their new neighbors. Nondivorced long-distance fathers can know that their children are being watched over not only by the children's mother, but also by neighbors, family, and friends.

Kids are walking, talking conversation pieces, and discussing them with your neighbors is a ready-made icebreaker. Many parents consider every day of their child's life fascinating and fuel for dialogue. If a father is willing to talk about children, he will never be in need of an introduction.

Dads striving to connect with other parents may find the following suggestions helpful:

- Take the initiative. Be the person who extends his hand and utters the first word. When you're home, this can be as simple as sitting next to another father at a T-ball game and saying, "Hello, I'm Steve, Stephany's dad. You're Ryan's father, aren't you?"

- Open up to the mothers of your child's friends. Ask how they feel about the local schools, the teachers, or child care.
- Speak *positively* about children, their interests, and upcoming events. When at sports activities, support all children, and congratulate other parents on *their* child's successes.
- Talk to other fathers about the challenges of co-parenting.
- If you're a road warrior or deployed dad, on days that you're home, drive your child to school and offer to take the neighbor's kid, too.
- Be patient. It takes time and shared experiences to create trust and camaraderie. This is especially true when a parent is screening a new acquaintance and taking care to avoid contact with undesirables.
- If you're a divorced dad living in a new place, meeting other parents could be a good way to find playmates for your youngster for when he or she comes to visit.
- Be optimistic; if you work to build relationships with other parents, you will either build or join a desirable community.

For children, their father's involvement with other parents means more opportunities to play. For parents, the greater the network, the easier it is to co-parent. The more people dads know, both at home and away, the easier it will be to find emotional and logistical support in the caring of their children.

Become Involved in School Activities

When you're the parent of a six- to ten-year-old, you may be just starting to realize how important school is in his or her young life. It's time for you to get involved, no matter where you live or how often you're away from home.

Federal law states that schools have to inform both parents of a child's activities and grades if they don't live in the same house. You should get this information in order to stay connected in your child's life. If you drop off some self-addressed, stamped envelopes for this purpose, you'll score major points with the often budget-challenged school and show that you are committed to being involved in your child's life.

Staying Involved with Their Teachers from Afar

Fathers can meet with teachers and principals when they're home or e-mail them while they're away. Most teachers these days have e-mail to connect with students and even have Web sites with upcoming events and homework. Find out what the school or classroom's homepage is and stay connected. You can request a phone conference with the teacher if you'll be away from home during conference time or if you have any questions for him or her regarding your child.

Chaperoning Field Trips

Looking back, it seems that the more school field trips I went on, the quicker I was accepted by my daughter's teachers and other parents. Being packed on a bus with thirty kids and half a dozen parents can certainly help to build camaraderie. If taking a class of fourth graders on an overnight trip won't help build unity between parents, then nothing will. Schools often have a shortage of male chaperones, so if you can work out your schedule to be there for your child, do so. At the beginning of the year, talk to the teacher and find out about the scheduling of these class trips so that you can make your schedule fit. Generally, if you explain your situation and express a desire to be involved—and a willingness to meet teachers halfway—you'll be well received. If you can't pin down your schedule to be there for a class trip, ask the teacher if you can volunteer in the classroom sporadically. That way, if your business trip lasts longer than expected or you find yourself home for several days with no plans, you can go in and help around the classroom. This could be doing anything from reading to the kids to teaching them something specific that you do in your career. Teachers always appreciate the extra help around the classroom, and if you come prepared, even better!

8

Children Ages Eleven to Fifteen

I HAVE A NUMBER OF FRIENDS WHO WORK IN education—administrators, teachers, and paraprofessionals—and one thing on which they all agree is the fact that what many of us refer to as the "middle school years" is often the most difficult period of adjustment in a child's life. In fact, children's brains will undergo more rapid growth and change during their fourteenth year than at any other time in their life aside from their first year.

This can make it difficult enough for a child; now throw in the fact that Mom and Dad are getting a divorce or that Dad is going to be away on business or deployed overseas.

Have I got your attention? I thought so.

Children Age Eleven to Fifteen: Characteristics and Specific Needs

If you're living through your child's transition from preteen to teenager, you'll no doubt recognize these signs: growth spurts (with a need to sleep for what seems to be eighteen hours per day); mood swings (especially with your daughters); the development of a sarcastic sense of humor; the apparent need to question not just everything you do, but your reasoning for doing it, and so on. They do grow up so fast, don't they?

What doesn't change for your kids during this monumental shift in their physical, mental, and emotional makeup is your kids' continuing need for you not only to be a constant in their life, but also for you to be consistent in your approach to your relationship with them.

I can attest to this from personal experience. I was in this age group when my parents separated. My father, hopeless about his life, the direction of his failed marriage, and wallowing in a morass of alcohol and shame, tragically took his own life. I was devastated. Because children at this age are easing from childhood into adulthood, they need a role model, someone to show them what it's like to be an adult. Without consistent contact with their dad, kids have less of an opportunity to see what a good adult looks and acts like and what behavior they should be modeling their own after.

Dads who are on the road need to be involved with their kids of this age to be aware of what their kids are exposing themselves to. There's a need for you to have a pulse on the finger of your child's life so that you know what risks they may be getting themselves into, because this is the age group where peer pressure to make bad decisions often happens. The consistency of a sense of security in knowing that their father is there for them, even if he's not in town, is much needed for kids of this age. Call home and ask about these issues. Ask what's happening in school; ask if your kids have been exposed to drugs. Say, "I want you to know that I'm available to give you my understanding of these subjects." All children that age want to know that there is someone setting the boundaries and watching out for them, even if you're not physically there.

First the Bad News (and Some Statistics)

In a *Time* magazine article titled, "The Price of a Broken Home," Judith Wallerstein reports the results of studying 131 children whose parents were divorcing: "Eighteen months after the breakup . . . we didn't see a single child that was well adjusted. And we didn't see a single child to whom divorce was not the central event of their lives . . . We realized that the whole trajectory of the child's life changes. Over half of the [now grown] children I have been studying have psychological problems they attribute to divorce."

Judith Wallerstein's conclusions have long been corroborated by more statistically comprehensive studies. Princeton's Sarra McLanahan, a recognized expert in social studies, found that "children of divorce drop out of high school, became teen mothers [and fathers], and are jobless far more frequently than their peers." Experts like Wallerstein and McLanahan bring to our attention some of the by-products of divorce—children unable to succeed in society, and young adults crippled in their attempts at love.

Currently in the United States, according to the Coalition of Parental Support (COPS), eighteen million children live in single-parent households. The following statistics were supplied by COPS. The first set deals with young women raised in fatherless families:

- 71 percent of teenage pregnancies are to children of single parents.

- Daughters of single parents are 2.1 times more likely to have children during their teenage years than are daughters from intact families.
- Daughters of single parents are 53 percent more likely to marry as teenagers.

Young men, like their female peers, are also at risk when raised in fatherless families. The following statistics are for young men and women:

- 90 percent of all homeless and runaway children are from fatherless homes.
- 75 percent of all adolescent patients in chemical abuse centers come from fatherless homes.
- 63 percent of youth suicides are from fatherless homes.
- 85 percent of all youths incarcerated grew up in fatherless homes.

Today, the percentage of marriages ending in divorce is almost twice that of 1968, the year my parents separated. Using the *Statistical Abstract of the United States*, 1960 through 1994, we can see a progressive disintegration of the family as shown by the increase in divorce and annulment. In 1910, 8.75 percent of marriages ended in divorce; in 1930, 17.39 percent of unions failed; in 1960, 25.80 percent of all marriages failed; and in 1990, 48 percent of those who said they would remain together later changed their minds. In 1992, according to *Time*, 2.3 million couples married and 1.2 million couples divorced. The U.S. Census Bureau currently projects six out of ten first marriages will end in divorce.

The Good News

It doesn't have to be as bad as the statistics above show. Keep in mind, those numbers are all for teens growing up in fatherless homes—where the father was not present in the teen's life in any way. You control a good portion of whether you will remain deeply involved in your children's lives regardless of your physical proximity to them (or lack thereof). Larry is a long-haul trucker who is gone from home for weeks at a time. Although his son Matt (currently age twelve) is able to join him on trips during school vacations, Larry and his wife, Jan, don't let it rest at just that. They make a point of letting Matt know where Larry is at any given time. Larry sits down with Matt before every trip and shows him on a map what route he'll be taking for that trip. They then get online and take a virtual look at the places Larry will be visiting, and they talk about those aspects of these places that interest Matt. They make lists of places they would like to visit together during Matt's school vacations, and so on. All of this stems from the choice of the family to actively parent, regardless of the physical distance between father and son.

Three Problems Facing Parents of Eleven- to Fifteen-Year-Olds

Here are three of the most pressing problems for fathers attempting to parent children in this age bracket:

1. Dealing with your child's shifting view of both you and the world around him or her.
2. Helping your child deal with the changes he or she is experiencing at this age level.

3. Maintaining a healthy, respectful relationship with your burgeoning teenager.

There's no question that these are thorny issues. Each one by itself can be tough enough to deal with, let alone all three together. Add divorce or physical separation into the mix and you're looking at a difficult road ahead for you and your kid.

As a long-distance dad, your relationship with your child can be just as fruitful as the bond fathers who see their children every evening are apt to have. How? Simple. Again, for the record, note that I said "simple," not "easy." There is a difference!

One thing that kids in this age group share with children in other age groups is a *craving for structure*. So it's up to you as one-half of their parents to do your best to establish a routine, a pattern, a set of immutable rules and to *stick with it*.

Also, kids this age are just beginning to figure out that there really are different sets of rules for adults than there are for kids. This is a potential minefield when they hit their late teens (and we will address those potential complications in Chapter 9), but for now there are some relatively simple solutions for this and the two other major problems you're likely to experience with your child in this age group.

Three Solutions

As I said before, structure is important, and in many ways, it's the foundation (no pun intended) of your continued strong relationship with your eleven- to fifteen-year-old. Let's put it in the mix with two other potential solutions to these daunting problems:

1. *Structure, structure, structure!* If your kids know what the schedule is, and what to expect from you as far as

rules and the like are concerned, they're likely to accept their existing situation as "normal," and sometimes getting your kids invested in good habits is really half the battle.

2. *Realistic rules.* Although there will always be certain things that parents are allowed to do that their kids aren't (and shouldn't be) allowed to do, there are certain rules that ought to be in force for every family member. It's up to you to decide what they should be; the important thing is that you make them and live by them as equally and as fully as you insist your children do. Not only does this set an example for them, but it's also what educational professionals call modeling appropriate behavior. For all of the sarcasm inherent in conversation with kids this age, they're not just watching you so they can point out your shortcomings. What you do still does count with kids in this age group, no matter how they let on otherwise. So if you make a universal rule against hitting, for example, hold yourself to it as much as you would them. "You cannot hit others, and I, the parent, cannot hit you." Be fair with them, and this, too, will be successful modeling.

3. *Patience is the watch word.* Remember, as if being a child of an absentee parent weren't tough enough, your kid is also going through incredible changes as he or she becomes a teenager. While it might be tempting to fly off the handle when your kid is getting on your last nerve, again, you're modeling for him or her, and this includes being able to show how adults handle frustration (such as the type that comes from having to say, "Because I *told* you to, that's why!" for the one-millionth time).

Nowhere will this be more necessary for you to exercise than when disciplining your kids. Don't get me wrong—when I say that you need to be consistent and patient, the last thing I mean is that you ought to be lenient or reluctant to discipline your children. Far from it. If you're a doormat, your kids will sense it, and they will walk all over you. What's more, if you and their mother aren't on the same page discipline-wise, this is the age at which your kids will start to play you off against each other, and you'll be the last person to know it.

Think I'm kidding? Think again. They may already be doing it to you. It's part of this stage of development, after all.

You can't do any of this if you're not an active part of your child's upbringing, which is all the more reason why you and your ex must be able to agree to parent as a team, even if you no longer cohabitate. I've said it before, and I'll say it again: if you're divorced, getting along with your ex (like consistently and patiently modeling appropriate behavior to your kids) pays enough dividends in the long term that it's worth your investment in the short term (and your kid's childhood is precisely that: the short term. I don't need to tell you that kids grow up fast!).

Oh, and being an active part of your child's upbringing doesn't mean just doling out discipline. Read the "She Says" sidebar on the next page for one mother's story of how her ex has never been to the city where she and their fifteen-year-old son live, and the sort of effect it's had on him.

Just because you don't live in the area doesn't mean that you can't and shouldn't visit. Quite the contrary! Your investment here is in your children, not in a place. And besides, who wants to be the one doling out the grief (discipline) and forgoing the gravy (getting to see your kid make an open-field tackle, recover a fumble, and run it back for the game-winning touchdown)?

She Says

Irene lives in Boston with her fifteen-year-old son, Justin. She moved there six years ago from California to take advantage of a terrific job opportunity. Justin has settled in well, plays football, has girls calling the house all the time, and is pretty well adjusted. There is something missing from his life, though. Irene explains: "Jeffrey [Justin's dad] has never been to Boston. He's never been to Justin's house; he's never seen his room. He's never been to one of Justin's soccer or football games, not one, and Justin has been playing sports here since the fourth grade. Justin still spends his summers and part of winter breaks with his father, but my father, Justin's grandfather, who is retired and lives in Las Vegas, is more involved in our son's life than his own father. His grandfather has come to his games—but his father has not. How sad is that, and not just for Justin, but for Jeff? The guy has no idea what he's missing."

So make this sort of investment in your kid. Find a way to be there for the important things. Know what his room looks like, know who his friends are. Be your child's ally through this process of growing up. Be your kid's father!

Working Together for the Good of All

Yet another reason both parents must be self-sufficient is that it makes it easier for them to develop the rapport necessary to work as a team. According to Wallerstein and Kelly's *Surviving the Breakup*, 50 percent of mothers see no value in the father's continued contact with the children after separation. Stanford Braver, in the *American Journal of Orthopsychiatry*, 1991, states that 40 percent of mothers respond that they had interfered with the noncustodial father's visitation on at least one occasion in order to punish the ex-spouse.

Divorced couples should work to lessen the impact of negative change on their families. For the good of all, parents who find themselves incapable of living together now need to provide two independent homes to care for their kids. Doing so will demonstrate to their children that both parents are committed, capable, and loving adults.

With women wanting the opportunity to have well-rounded lives, and fathers eager for the opportunity to co-parent, the equal sharing of parental responsibility after divorce is an idea that fits the times. Unfortunately, there are fathers who are afraid to parent, women who do not want to take on financial roles, judges with outmoded ideas, and counselors who view men as inept caregivers for children.

The theme of working together for the good of all—that sense of teamwork—that's what fathers need to instill in their family. If you're always reinforcing that idea with your wife or ex-wife and your children, then when challenges come up, and they will, that's what the father can always fall back on. No matter what's going on, you can say to your children, "I want you to know that we're all in this together and we're all going to figure out a way to come out the other side."

It's important to present a united front with your children's mom as a team. Always say, "Your mother and I will handle this." Set a high yet realistic standard for your children by doing this. It's important for fathers who are not always at home to not delegate their authority to the mother. It's also bad to adopt the mother's parenting style because she's home more often. Mothers appreciate differing parenting styles and you remaining consistent in yours. They want a partnership. Communicate together before presenting a punishment or rule to your child so that you are united.

Remember, with your kids at this age, you and their mother owe them (and yourself) patience, consistency, active parenting, and involvement, involvement, involvement. The good news? These four years will fly by! The challenging news? Your kid is about to turn sixteen. So, when you reach the end of this stage of your child's development, you will deserve a pat on the back.

9

Children Ages Sixteen to Twenty

SO YOU'RE THE PARENT OF A TEENAGER. TALK about challenging! One moment you've got a kid who just wants to be told what to do next, and the next moment you've got a mouthy know-it-all who is all too willing to not only tell *you* what to do, but also to list each and every one of your myriad faults for you in excruciating detail, while in the next breath telling you to mind your own damned business where their personal lives are concerned.

In a recent *New York Times* review of an art exhibition at the Whitney Museum, *Times* art critic Holland Cotter wrote the following about teenagers: "Young people are by definition narcissistic, all clammy ego. They want what they want. There is no past that matters; the future isn't yet real."

Sound familiar? While it's true that certain aspects of parenting a teenager can be challenging, it's important for you as an active parent to realize that this is a necessary time for them. Teenagers are becoming self-aware and are learning to think for themselves. They are also beginning the natural process of creating an identity for themselves independent of their parents and the family unit.

Unfortunately, since they begin this process with no experience, they start out really terrible at it. So there are cross words, moodiness, and false note after false note sounded as they practice being their own person and establishing their own identity.

One Long-Distance Dad's Creative Solution to Parenting a Teen

Russ, a professional musician who was divorced shortly after his daughter Erin turned fifteen, remembers the adjustments required not just by the change in the family's circumstances, but by the changes in Erin's behavior. "Because I play sax for a living, I'm no stranger to the types of substances frequently used and abused in musical circles. Erin has been a music lover with a talent for singing since she could crawl. When Valerie and I began having trouble, my daughter went 'Goth' and started to act out by wearing black, curling her lip, and shrugging at the most innocuous of questions. I was also pretty sure that she had begun to experiment with ecstasy."

Formally separated and on tour at the time, Russ was doubly a long-distance dad in that he was not cohabitating with his family, and he was on the road three weeks out of every four. According to Russ, part of the reason for their split was because Valerie didn't support him in his attempts to discipline Erin (a common enough complaint in many marriages today), and he wound up feeling as if he was always "the bad guy."

Not surprisingly, when Russ was around and able to talk to his daughter, she tended to behave in a sullen and withdrawn manner. She began talking about things like tattoos, obviously intent on getting some sort of shock value out of these statements. Russ handled this in an innovative way: he convinced Valerie to agree to let him take his sixteen-year-old daughter on the road with him.

That's right: she had been talking so much about living an "alternative lifestyle" that he took matters into his own hands and showed her one! According to Russ, "Erin was ready to head home the first time she had to do laundry. Not just her own, but mine as well. And if she got it wrong, she didn't get any allowance. We had a battle of wills for a few days, but the grind and my patience wore her out."

Today Erin is also a musician. She sings opera (of all things!), and her jazz musician father is finding enough of an appreciation for it that he's there in the audience every time his touring schedule allows him to be. They get along well, and Erin's relationship with her mother is also stronger as a result of the risk that Russ took so many years ago.

Children Age Sixteen to Twenty: Characteristics and Specific Needs

We've already laid out some specifics of this age group, but let's review quickly. Kids of this age are trying to assert their independence, and it shows in their behavior. They can be sullen, opinionated, sarcastic, self-centered, and extremely narcissistic. As for their needs, they remain similar to their needs during the previous five years of development. These kids need structure, patience, and understanding. More than that, they need room to spread their wings,. This is no easy proposition for any involved parent. So that begs the question: How to go about this?

Three Problems Facing Parents of Sixteen- to Twenty-Year-Olds

Here are three of the most common problems cited by dads of kids in this age group:

1. Dealing with the fallout from their kids' physiological changes as they advance into young adulthood. This includes, but is not limited to, having a child who is constantly threatening to move away permanently and live with the other parent as a means of getting his or her way on this or that issue. Teenagers are just learning how to be truly manipulative, and it can often manifest itself in petty, ham-handed tactics such as these.
2. Being able to give your kids enough space to be themselves (or in fact to find out who they are in the first place) without letting go of your obligation to be responsible for them.
3. Teen dating!

Of course these three problems don't ever present themselves singly. In fact, they usually come as a package deal. Now here's how you deal with them.

Three Solutions

There's no magic bullet here. As with your actions in your children's previous stages of development, you're going to be called on to be patient and involved, thusly:

1. Continue to be available and attentive when your child makes the effort to communicate with you. The relationship you've labored so hard to build up to this point will

not only stand you in good stead now, but it will also continue to be enhanced by this active reliance upon it.

2. Make sure that you are still actively parenting your kid, no matter that he or she is almost an adult. After all, you never stop being a parent; you just stop being legally responsible when they turn eighteen. Do everything you can to help prepare your child for adulthood. This includes allowing him or her to screw up from time to time, and also letting your child get him- or herself out of the scrapes all teens get into at one time or another. After all, your child can't learn to be self-reliant if he or she is always relying on you. That doesn't mean that you can't help your children (after all, they *are* your kids!), it just means that you're going to need to be willing to allow them to learn from their mistakes.

3. Every father should have a safe-sex discussion with his child to prepare him or her for adulthood. Fathers are not going to be aware of every detail of their children's dating life, so they need to prepare their children by having a talk. Don't be afraid to ask in a matter-of-fact, loving, and truly interested way if they are dating. Ask your children how involved they are, how involved they think they should be, and what they think is appropriate for people their age. You can have this conversation from anywhere in the country, via the phone, a letter, or virtual visitation. You're not entitled to every detail— children are entitled to their privacy. End every conversation with words of appreciation—tell your kids that you're there if they want to discuss anything. Don't just assume that since you're gone their mother has had this talk with them. Fathers need to overcome the myth that

these talks are best left to mothers. Even if it's awkward, the stakes are too high not to have the talk just because you're uncomfortable. Talk to their mother and other fathers who have gone through this and figure out the best way for you to approach it.

No one ever said that parenting a teenager was easy. After all, if raising healthy, well-adjusted kids were easy, then anyone could do it!

Peer Pressure for Teens

In every school, city, and state there is peer pressure among teens to do what it takes to be accepted and admired. Being accepted is especially important to adolescents as their lives and bodies are changing; to face these changes without the support of their peers seems unthinkable. Making life more challenging is the fact that the brains of teens are not fully developed physically, so teens may lack the good judgment that more developed minds are capable of. Now add to the teen challenge the fact that there are fellow students who smoke pot, abuse alcohol, and are engaging in sex. What you have is an environment where peer pressure can be very convincing and effective.

Now combine the three ingredients—peer pressure to do what is "cool," plus adolescent minds apt to make immature choices, plus a sprinkling of kids in the student body who already indulge in risky behavior—and you see the minefields teens navigate in order to become adults. It is a daunting task, and those without a connection to their fathers lack a valuable resource.

Fathers can present the logic needed by their children to overcome peer pressure. A family discussion about the consequences of unsafe sex, alcoholism, drug addiction, depression, and running away from home can save lives. Most teens will appreciate the father's willingness to assist them as they struggle to grow up, especially if the long-distance dad is understanding and a good listener. Most teens walk a thin line; on one side of the road they want the support of their parents and on the other side they want the world to view them as self-sufficient. Fortunately, most kids know both that they present a challenge—immature minds, raging hormones, and attitude—and that in spite of it, their fathers love them and stand beside them.

Finding Activities to Enjoy with Your Young Adult

As I mentioned in a previous chapter, it's important to find something that both of you enjoy doing together. Because your child is now nearing adult age, this activity can be something that you enjoy in your adult life, be it going to the movies; attending concerts; fishing; hiking; playing pool, board games, chess; what have you. Maybe it's playing or watching (or even just talking about) sports. Several years ago, a character in the movie *City Slickers* said of his otherwise strained relationship with his father, "There was always baseball. No matter what, we could always talk baseball." Whatever activity you settle on, make sure it's something that you both enjoy doing, and make it a priority: something that you two will have together and for which you both set aside time in your schedule. It's shared activities like this that help build a bond between father and child far more than handing your kid the keys to his or her first car or paying for his or her college ever will.

10

Adult Children

YOUR CHILD IS NOW AN ADULT. BUT THE JOB OF parenting is not over. Rather, it is time to start a difficult transition wherein you increasingly take on the role of supportive friend, a good listener, and, when called upon, an adviser. Of course, there may well be need to be of some financial support for professional training, purchasing a house, or moving across the country to that first big job.

In this day and age, your kid is more likely to go away either to college or the military than stick around your house once he or she is over the age of twenty. So the question is: what do you do now?

The Myth of the Empty Nest

Let's face it; if you're sending a kid to college, you're going to see him or her: either at holidays or when he or she comes home to do laundry (or some combination thereof!). What's more, when your kids have kids, they're going to give you a prime opportunity not only to continue to connect with them (usually through offering them child care), but also to connect with a whole new generation—your grandkids!

So, realistically, how likely are you to see your kids once they've moved out? That depends on what sort of relationship you've built with them up to this point. If you've done the heavy lifting of being there during their formative years, your kids are likely to want to continue to preserve that relationship, albeit in a slightly different form.

Adult Children: Characteristics and Specific Needs

Adult children come in all shapes and sizes and every age over twenty. So unlike with our other age/development-specific sections, we won't be talking about what your average twenty-three-year-old needs. Instead, we'll talk about how to best allow the baseline relationship you've established with your kids to develop into a healthy adult relationship with them. First, remember, it's all about respect. Give it, be consistent, and you get it. This is where all those years of treating your kid with respect (especially when disciplining them) really starts to pay off. After all, you've given it and insisted on getting it in return for so long by now that it's ingrained in your kids to operate on this level with you, regardless of the potential rebelliousness of their teen years.

Three Problems Facing Parents of Adults

Here are three areas with which parents of adult children struggle:

1. Parents experiencing difficulty in "letting go" of their adult kids

2. One parent getting sucked into a difficulty between their adult kid and the other parent
3. Parents and their relationship with their adult kids who have children of their own

Let's face it: letting go can be tough. After all, it seems like just yesterday that you were putting a Band-Aid on the knee of that up-and-coming young stockbroker with the corner office. Of course, your kids see it differently, and unfortunately for you, they're right. Sometimes we as parents have a difficult time letting our kids be adults. We catch ourselves lecturing them about things they're perfectly capable of figuring out for themselves. We develop a tendency to start sentences with words like "You just need to . . ." and the next thing you know, we're talking to them in the same manner in which our own parents drove us to distraction during our twenties, thirties, forties, and so on.

Or worse still, we find ourselves acting as the referee between our kids and their mother. Since our kids are grown now, it's important to realize when we have to stop co-parenting, and when they're adults and we have done our job well enough that they're capable of thinking for themselves, it's likely time to stop presenting the all-important "united front" with their mother if she's intent on infantilizing them.

Lastly, the first problem we cited above can tie in with the last one when we start talking to our kids about how they're raising their own kids. After all, we're the experts, and we can be a resource to them if only they'll let us. This is, of course, not true.

Three Solutions
Here are three simple (again, not "easy") solutions to these dilemmas:

1. Learn to let go. You raised your kids right. Show that you have faith in them. Remind them that you're proud of them. Granted, they'll make mistakes—we all do. But let them make them; this is their life, their adventure. Let them enjoy it.

2. If you're divorced, you'll probably not be in as much communication with your children's mother as they grow older. You no longer have to arrange for child support, and so on. Where you used to have to communicate with her often, now you may not see her until a family event arises. You're two separate people who have worked together to raise great kids. By allowing your children's mother to chart her own way with your kids, you're also continuing to respect her and her choices, even when you don't agree with them.

3. When it comes to your grandchildren, the best thing you can do (aside from being involved in their lives) is to shut up and let your kids come to you with parenting questions. If you don't volunteer your opinion all the time, odds are good that your kids will feel comfortable coming to you for the advice you're dying to give. Also, don't undermine your kids in their attempts to be good parents. For example, if they have decided to limit their child's access to sweets, you have no business feeding your grandkid chocolate when he or she comes to visit.

Don't Undermine Your Child's Parenting Skills

What if (God forbid!) your kid is divorced and is struggling with co-parenting his or her own kids? If you've established a solid relationship with your kid, you will likely be able to offer advice, since he or she has seen firsthand how good you are at it. However, every situation is different, every kid is different, and every parent is different. Remember to keep it aboveboard, keep the lines of communication open (without being "invasive"), and let your kids be adults. Harder than it sounds, I know, but after all, if you'd had it all figured out when you became a parent, you wouldn't have made the brilliant decision to read this book!

Being a Long-Distance Grandfather

Maybe you're one of these long-distance granddads. In America, as opposed to in Europe, there is not the trend for adult children to stay close to their parents to raise their own children. It is likely that you will find yourself being a long-distance granddad. You may even find yourself sometimes acting as a surrogate parent (frequently a long-distance one) who provides both emotional and financial support for his grandchildren who lack an immediate male role model in their lives for a variety of reasons.

He Says

Robert, a long-distance grandfather, says, "Because I'm a retired English instructor and writer, I enjoy picking out books that I think will match my grandchildren's interests. When we speak on the phone, we have something to say to one another and I, too, make it clear that I welcome suggestions about what it is they'd like me to read. One grandson is an aspiring poet/songwriter, and sends work from time to time, and asks for 'honest criticism.' I have a granddaughter, Maxine, who lives on the island of Grenada. I live in California, yet I want to be part of her life. My daughter tells me that, for Maxine, I am the grandfather who has helped her create a library."

If this role befalls you, accept it gladly and use the skills that you have learned as a long-distance dad in your new role of long-distance grandparenting. Visit your grandchildren as often as possible, use virtual visitation, and make it clear to your grand-kids that you will be there for them, even from a distance. Don't forget however, that you come second to your own child, their parent, in doling out the rules and discipline to your grandchil-dren. Have an attitude of cooperation with your child so that you are on the same page as to the needs of your grandchild. It's a team effort—although you're done parenting your own child, he or she may appreciate the time you have to devote to his or her child. A helping hand is always appreciated, and it's never a case of either/or; it's both the grandparent and the parent being there for the child. Be in your grandchildren's lives as much as they, and your own child, need you to be.

11

Taking Advantage of Technology

ALMOST EVERYONE HAS SEEN A SCIENCE-FICTION movie that shows a parent communicating using a "video call" to talk with his or her children. The astronauts from the Apollo space program did this in the 1960s, just as we saw it on *Star Trek*. In the 1980s we had *Star Wars*; in the 1990s we saw "video calling" in many movies and television shows depicting the future.

Well, the future is here! Today, we can use text messaging, instant messaging, and video calling to stay in touch with our children. We can do so whether they are around the corner, across town, across the country, or across the world.

Text Messaging and Instant Messaging

Any tool that helps a father stay connected to his children is a great idea. Text messages on the cell phone and instant messages on the computer are both ways to stay in touch with your children when you're crunched for time or want to send a quick reminder that you love them.

Text Messaging

Basically all cell phones these days come with a text messaging, or "SMS," feature. When you set up your phone and your child's phone (if they have one), ask the provider how much individual text messages cost or how much it would cost to add a text messaging package onto your plan. Usually text messages are very inexpensive, about ten cents each.

The more advanced the phone, the more options you have for texting—with some phones you can send a picture message and even a video message! This is a great way for dads to send very brief messages to their children as reminders that they are thinking of them and are still interested in their lives from afar. A quick message to say "Hope you're having a great day! Love, Dad" is a good reminder to your child that you are there for them even when you're away.

Some dads might be intimidated by typing out messages on the number pad of a phone—don't worry, the more you do this, the more you will get used to it. Some kids these days can text faster than they can talk (hard to believe, I know!) but you don't need to try to keep up with them. You can ask your child to help you learn the abbreviations that many kids use in both texting and instant messaging—such as "LOL" for "laughing out loud" and "I<3U" for "I love you."

Instant Messaging

Unlike text messaging, instant messaging is not something that you can do quickly while you're out and about. Because you must be sitting at a computer in order to send instant messages back and forth with your child, why not video chat or talk on the phone instead? Instant messaging can be a useful tool for long-distance fathers, however, in situations when they are at a computer but unable to talk on the phone. For instance, if you sit at a computer during work, you could have the instant messaging window open so that your child knows that if he or she wants reassurance from you, he or she can get it. This depends partly on your ability to multitask and your company's policy on chat programs such as AIM, Yahoo Chat, and Gmail chat.

Remember that regardless of all of the advancements in technology, letters and postcards can be kept forever—any type of instant communication should never fully take the place of pen and paper or seeing your child in person.

Virtual Visitation and Its Uses

Virtual visitation has many names: virtual parent-time, Internet visitation, video phone, video call, computer visitation, and others. The common legal term is "virtual visitation," which we will use here, though it may vary from state to state or individual preference. It involves using tools such as personal video conferencing, a webcam, e-mail, instant messaging, and other wired or wireless technologies. There are certain times that virtual visitation is appropriate for use. These are:

- Divorced parents wanting to communicate with their children *and* one another
- Dads separated by distance (for whatever reason) wanting to communicate with their families
- Dads traveling on business or vacation wanting to keep in touch with other family members

- Grandparents wanting to communicate with distant family members, children, and grandchildren
- Children whose parents are overseas on military assignment
- Counseling centers that are facilitating parent-to-children communication
- Dads and teachers seeking an inexpensive tool for remote contact
- Parents wanting to make the most of their children's being so connected, including use of online chat programs, e-mail, video chat, cell phones, among others, in order to maximize their opportunities for communication with their kids

What virtual visitation is *not* appropriate for: use as a replacement or substitute for in-person contact with one's children. Some have expressed concerns that virtual visitation is intended to substitute for in-person or face-to-face visits with one's children. Not so. The most important contact you can have with your children is one-on-one, face-to-face. But when you can't be there, virtual visitation is a significant improvement over the telephone.

Virtual Visitation Benefits

Most informed men support legislation that will protect parents' rights and guide the courts as to the proper use of this technology. That is, to "supplement" in-person visits, not to replace them. This is technology that is available to all long-distance dads. For example, Dan read bedtime stories to his son via video call while he was deployed to Iraq.

Dan says, "I read *Wind in the Willows* to my son using virtual visitation. That is one of my favorite books and my son loves it too. You can't hold your kids and share one book. You can, though, laugh together. And turn the pages at the same time and show each other the pictures you like. My son and I loved the scene where Toad recaptures Toad Manor from the weasels and then Mole shouts his war cry, 'It's a mole, it's a mole.' That is priceless. We finished *Wind in the Willows* and I watched his eyes get sleepy. And just like when I'm with him, he says, 'I'm not sleepy' and falls asleep."

Virtual visitation also enables parents to confer more easily and for one parent to reinforce the decision of another. It can be used to visit with extended family members and, at the same time, help children feel they have two devoted and loving parents even though their father is away most or all of the time.

Virtual visits every evening can be a chance for you to read a bedtime story to your son or daughter. Typically, it works for moms of young kids too, as they get a break and the knowledge that dad is connecting with his kids. Virtual visits with toddlers can last longer than phone calls because kids can see their dads. Because Dad can see his child, he knows when his child falls asleep, and that signals the end of that night's bedtime reading. Now, Mom notices the silence, enters, turns off the computer and the lights, and enjoys the rest of her evening. Thanks, dear.

For older kids, virtual visitation allows fathers to assist with homework, give feedback on the daughter's new hair color, and see the kids' latest karate moves. Every long-distance dad should invest in virtual visitation; today's children are capable computer users, and you can and should be too.

Virtual Visitation Legislation

Michael Gough, nicknamed the "Father of Virtual Visitation," crusaded to help create the first bill, "Saige's Law" (named after his daughter), to add Virtual Visitation Amendments to the Utah divorce code, where it is now in effect. A Wisconsin law, "Electronic Communication," has also been passed, this one unanimously. Gough's efforts have led to legislation being considered in many other states, from California to Maine, and in 2007 he added Texas and Florida, where virtual visitation is now law. The goal of the legislation is to educate the courts, attorneys, and legal professionals who will, in turn, inform all concerned as to the benefits and just uses of virtual visitation in divorce and custody cases. The following information about virtual visitation comes from Michael's research and his *Virtual Visitation Handbook*.

Adding Virtual Visitation to Your Divorce Settlement

Courts are increasingly implementing virtual visitation in child-related cases, recognizing children's critical need to have both parents in their lives. Judges will not be able to ignore the new technology as they weigh conflicting pleas from divorced parents. Advocates of virtual visitation say communicating over the Internet is especially helpful in cases that involve supervised visits. It is also being used as a remedy for noncustodial parents to remain in contact with their children. Moreover, laws are being passed to implement virtual visitation as an automatic option, like the telephone.

Step One

The first step in getting virtual visitation into your divorce settlement is to know what is required and the approximate costs—$500 in 2007—associated with buying the equipment. See the "Equipment required" list that follows later.

Because this is a fairly new trend, you will probably need to have wording inserted into your divorce decree (see sample wording below).

For most current information on equipment and software, please check *www.InternetVisitation.org* and *www.VideoCallTips. com*. *The Virtual Visitation Handbook,* available free of charge at *www.InternetVisitation.org,* is updated as new hardware and software become available.

If you can, offer up the equipment as part of your divorce settlement. Doing so may prove far less expensive than litigating over $500. You might then be in a position to negotiate for the ongoing high-speed Internet charges.

Wording for Your Divorce Decree

Your legal counsel or attorney will help you adjust the wording to fit your specific state and situation.

Cooperative Relationship: For a cooperative relationship, a general order can suffice, such as, "The parties will cooperate to provide virtual visitation for the child with each parent."

High-Conflict Relationship: In high-conflict relationships, a tightly crafted order, with concrete specifications for implementation, can help make video calls a reality for the child.

POINTS TO INCLUDE IN THE ORDER

1. Which technologies are being ordered (video calls, e-mail, instant messaging, cell phone, video cell phone, etc.)
2. Equipment required:
   - ❏ PC or Apple computer
   - ❏ Quality webcam
   - ❏ Headset/microphone
   - ❏ Video call software

❏ High-speed Internet (Cable/DSL) connection (*Note:* In rural areas, a high-speed Internet connection may not be available. As of 2007, speeds through satellite connections are not yet adequate.)

❏ DSL/Cable broadband router (for security)

❏ Personal firewall software (for security and privacy)

❏ Virus and spyware protection (Windows)

3. Installation and training services if needed

4. Which parent is required to pay for necessary equipment and services. That is, who will provide and pay for:

    ❏ The needed equipment for the custodial parent

    ❏ The needed equipment for the noncustodial parent

    ❏ The monthly high-speed Internet connection for the custodial parent

    ❏ The monthly high-speed Internet connection for the noncustodial parent

5. Schedule: for example, days of the week, number of times per week, and times of day for virtual visitation to occur (we recommend an hour or so before bedtime for young children)

6. Which parent is responsible for initiating the virtual visitation session

7. Deadline for custodial parent to have equipment ready and video call in full operation

8. If equipment malfunctions, the acceptable time period allowed for computer repair before court sanctions are triggered

9. Remedies and sanctions for noncompliance, including contempt and attorney fees

Preparing to Fight for Virtual Visitation in Court

In the unfortunate case that you have to go to court to request virtual visitation, be prepared to convince the court that virtual visitation is valuable. Hopefully, you will not have to show a demonstration in court, but if you do, then this section will give you an idea of what is needed and how to prove to the court that virtual visitation is easy to set up and inexpensive to use.

Getting Started

Your legal counsel will help decide the proper approach, but the first three areas in the following list need to be covered:

- What you actually want
- Supporting documentation and existing laws and/or pending bills
- Articles on virtual visitation
- A demonstration if absolutely necessary

How You Want to Set It Up

Your counsel will assist you with the items that are appropriate to your case. For example:

1. How many times per week do you want to perform virtual visitation? This will depend on the age of the children. The older they are, the more they can initiate video calls without inconveniencing the custodial parent.
2. What days of the week will conferencing take place?
3. What will be the time of day for your calls?
4. What is the duration of the calls you expect to make?
5. Who will provide and pay for the computer or dedicated videophone device?

6. Who will provide and pay for the additional equipment (webcam and headset/microphone)?
7. Who will provide and pay for any required upgrades?
8. Who will provide and pay for the high-speed Internet connection?

You need to have a plan to address these questions before going to court. Be prepared to pay for all of it if you truly want virtual visitation. Your counsel can assist in guiding you on how both of your incomes come into play.

Demonstration in Court

If you feel a detailed plan of what you want and supporting documentation are not enough, then a courtroom demonstration may be required. For how to present a courtroom demonstration, see *The Virtual Visitation Handbook*.

What You Need in Your Home (or When Traveling) to Video Call with Your Family

The following will help answer your questions about virtual visitation once you've received agreements from your child's mom (or the courts) or for when you're traveling.

Broadband Internet Connection

The primary goal of selecting a high-speed Internet provider is to get an upload speed of at least 150kbps, preferably 200kbps or faster. If you can get cable television, then most likely you can get a high-speed cable modem from your cable provider. High-speed Internet from your cable provider is the fastest option available for the home user. If you cannot get cable, then ask other high-speed Internet providers what their "minimum guaranteed" speed is.

Recommendation: Cable modem

Broadband Router

A broadband router allows you to connect more than one computer to your high-speed connection or to use wireless Internet (Wi-Fi) within your home. A broadband router also provides a very good level of security to protect your system from malicious computer activity. Always consider a wireless version for your DSL/cable router so you have flexibility in using your computer anywhere in your home. We recommend getting a router with 4 or more ports and 802.11g or 802.11n wireless.

Recommendation: Wireless 802.11g or 802.11n DSL/cable router

Computer or No Computer

If one of the following reasons to get a dedicated video telephone device rather than buying a computer is applicable in your situation, then select a dedicated videophone device like the D-Link i2eye VideoPhone or dedicated video telephone services from Ojo or Packet8. Reasons for a dedicated video telephone device rather than a computer with a webcam include:

- Cost—you need the least-expensive solution and do not have a computer.
- You are using it for family members who are not comfortable using a computer.
- You are using it in an elderly care facility.
- You are in a divorce situation with children under five who are not yet computer-savvy and cooperation is an issue with the other parent.

Otherwise, a Macintosh or Windows PC will meet your needs. *Recommendation: Computer running Windows XP or Vista*

Intel-Based PCs versus Apple/Mac

If you're purchasing a new computer, keep in mind that many more options are available for the PC than the Mac, and most people you will communicate with will have a PC. However, if you already own a Mac or know you want to use a Mac on both sides, please take into account that AOL Instant Messenger (AIM Triton) supports communicating with Apple's iChat Audio Video (AV) solution. There are also solutions if one of you has a PC and one has a Mac—SightSpeed and Skype, for example.

Which Mac?

If you have a Mac, anything later than an Apple G4 should work fine. For traveling, I recommend Apple's MacBook Pro, released in 2006, which comes with a built-in iSight camera and iChat AV software. Apple's spiel says it all: "Just because you're a thousand miles away, there's no reason you can't attend the weekly staff meeting or read a bedtime story to your daughter. Not if you're traveling with a new MacBook Pro. With its built-in iSight camera and stellar iChat AV software, it provides everything you need to be face-to-face with family, friends, colleagues, or clients in just a few minutes."

Webcams for PC and Mac

Many webcams will work fine. The top choices for PCs are:

- Logitech QuickCam series
- Logitech QuickCam for notebooks Pro series
  Recommendation: Logitech QuickCam ($100 version or better)

For Macs the choices are:

- Apple iSight (built-in)
  Recommendation: Apple iSight

Headset/Microphone

A combination headset/microphone is the same for the PC or the Mac. In making your decision, consider how it fits and what it costs. Use a headset/microphone designed to plug in to your computer's audio card. They have two ⅛-inch plugs, one pink (microphone) and one green (headphone) connector. The following headset/microphone manufacturers are among the best:

- Plantronics
- Altec Lansing
- Logitech

You may also use computer speakers with a noise-canceling microphone instead of a headset for a hands-free experience. Turn down the volume on the speakers when you are making a video call so the other side does not encounter echo or feedback.

Recommendation: Headset or speaker/microphone combination

Personal Video Call Solutions for the Windows PC

Select one of the free solutions to start. Later you can evaluate other options depending on your needs.

- Microsoft Windows Live Messenger
- Skype
- SightSpeed
  Recommendation: Any of the above

Personal Video Call Solutions for the Apple

As with the PC, select one of the free solutions to start and evaluate others depending on your needs.

- SightSpeed (Windows and Mac)
- Skype (Windows and Mac)
- Apple iChat AV
  Recommendation: Any of the above

Considerations for Successful Video Calls

- **Lighting.** Lighting is a crucial component for a successful video call. For optimal background color, conduct the video call under fluorescent lights. Direct sunlight is too bright and will wash out your face. Make sure your webcam faces away from an open window. Lighting should light up your face; a desktop light works well for this.
- **Eye contact.** During a video call, look straight at the computer monitor or the lens of the webcam.
- **Clothing.** Blue or dark green solid shirts are ideal. Try to avoid loud prints and stripes as well as black and white shirts since they absorb and reflect light, making the wearer look pale.
- **Chair position.** Sit in the middle of the chair. Because this is visual communication, posture is important. Try to sit straight, with your chair positioned in front of the webcam.

Online Security and Privacy

Securing your Internet connection and your computer from malicious activity is essential. A DSL/cable router or broadband router as they are also called is recommended in addition to personal firewall software (e.g., Norton Internet Security).

Personal Firewall Software

In selecting a personal firewall solution, consider what parental controls you might wish to invoke. For added security, all webcams come with a lens cover that you can use when the webcam is not in use. The lens can also be turned so it is not "looking" into the room or space. And, of course, it can be unplugged when not in use.

Recommendation: Symantec's Norton Internet Security Suite

Protecting Children from Internet Predators

Recently, in a December *New York Times* article and on a January 2006 *Oprah* show, child predators and pedophiles were discussed, showing the worst possible thing that could happen if a child is left to use a computer and the Internet unattended—the key term being "unattended."

Predators prey on children, in person or using the Internet, to exploit them for a variety of reasons. These people present themselves to your children or find your children through chat rooms (IRC) or personal Web sites like *www.myspace.com, www.me.com*, and other personal information portals.

Privacy in Social Networking Sites

Children are placing information about themselves on the Internet via Web sites like *www.myspace.com, www.facebook.com*, and *www.me.com*, and many parents have no idea what their children are placing on such sites or what their children are actually doing on their computer at any given time. Recently a school in Wisconsin went to *www.myspace.com* and collected information about their students and sent the information home to their parents. The information the district found shocked many, and this has caused a lot of discussion to occur on the subject of "What is my child actually doing on the Internet?"

Safe Surfing

In the computer security business, a common saying is "Trust but Verify." In computer security this is more than a saying, it is a driving force behind how we do our line of work. Our children should be no different. If you have given your child permission to use the Internet, you should also accept the parental responsibility of monitoring your child's Internet activity.

Of course, we support using webcams for virtual visitation. Adding a webcam to your computer does not, by itself, add any additional risk to you or your children. The risk is unmonitored activity. Most webcam vendors offer lens covers, and you can always turn the webcam sideways, away from the living space, when not in use, or even unplug it and put it away.

The bottom line: If you connect your computer to the Internet and let your children use it, you as a parent have an obligation to monitor their activity. Again, good in theory, but we all know that we cannot watch our children's Internet activity 24–7 . . . or can we? (Answer: Yes, we can.)

Please see *www.InternetVisitation.org* for more information on how to protect your computer and how to protect your children from predators as they use the Internet and practice virtual visitation. You can learn how to monitor your children's Internet access and help teach or guide them how to surf the Internet safely. As good as the *New York Times* and *Oprah* were to show you how scary things can be, they failed to tell you there are ways to reduce or virtually eliminate these risks.

It is up to you, the parent, to make sure your children do not fall prey to the scary things that can happen on the Internet, just as you must watch over them in everyday life. Monitor your children's Internet access with the information we provided and you can sleep at night knowing your children are using the Internet for learning and communication and avoiding the issues that can endanger them.

Lastly, don't forget that all of the technology in the world won't help you attain virtual visitation without the cooperation of the mother of your children. So what you should do is use the solid system of communication that you have already established with her in order to show her how allowing this sort of interaction on her part will help make for more well-rounded kids in both your households. Please contact *www.InternetVisitation. org* if you have any questions or need assistance with your case.

12

Your Kids' Mom:
Your Ally in Parenting

"This sort of relationship is like any other relationship: it begins and ends with respect."
—Barry, divorced long-distance father

BARRY HAS IT RIGHT. SAY IT WITH ME, SHOUT IT with me, live it with me! It's *all* about respect. The key to successfully navigating the shoals of a long period of separation from your kids (because of divorce, separation, work-related absences, etc.) while still raising healthy, happy, well-adjusted children is to keep this word in mind. Not just respect for the mother of your children, but respect for yourself (because no one wants to deal with a self-pitying, passive-aggressive doormat), and for the ongoing relationship itself.

Common Problems and Solutions

Here, more than anywhere else, is where most fathers trip up. There are a variety of reasons, but many men aren't able to separate what issues they may have with their wives/

girlfriends/exes from their desire to play an active role in the raising of their children. Try doing a bit of research on your own. In this age of the nontraditional family (to say nothing of divorce), here are a few simple suggestions that will help you communicate better with the mother of your kids in order to attain your goal of achieving maximum positive involvement in your kids' life:

- Treat her the way you'd like to be treated. Easy to say, sometimes tough to practice.
- Remember to breathe.
- Count to ten before responding to something that really pushes your buttons.
- E-mail is a great way to both force you to be objective about what you're saying and how you're saying it and to create a record of your interactions. Use it.
- Keep your interactions as businesslike and focused on the kids as possible.
- *Repeat for emphasis:* Keep it about your kids!

Note that we've kept the above set of recommendations general in order to be helpful for long-distance dads of all backgrounds and living situations, married, separated, or divorced.

Good Parenting Through Good Communication

First of all, you *must* have the assistance of your child's mother in good communication. There is no way around it.

If you're divorced (or never married and not cohabitating), it is incumbent on you to convince your child's mother that it is in your kids' best interest to have their father involved in their life as much as possible, and in every meaningful way available. For you divorced/nonmarried dads, this is part and parcel of the reason why we so strongly emphasized the notion of treating your child's mother with respect, regardless of whether or not you think she deserves it. In the long run, you benefit your child most of all, and yourself as a close second.

Those who are committed to creating a co-parenting relationship must move past the defensive, angry father's point of view. Men who are successful in doing so learn to look at the larger picture, realizing that their case will not be won or lost on any given day. They abandon their fears and, instead, learn to act and speak from a place of steady determination.

Once the initial shock of the divorce has passed, such men abandon the role of frustrated victim and become more grounded in who they really are as men and fathers—kindhearted, open-minded, and confident. The first step in the transition, of course, is to get rid of one's anger. Once one has moved beyond anger, one can view a situation and the larger world from a broader perspective.

Aids for Communication

A co-parenting couple will, in the years ahead of them, have numerous opportunities to use the communication skills in this chapter. To refresh your memory, and before each potentially difficult encounter, review the steps outlined below:

- Know in advance of the meeting with your child's mother what it is you want to achieve.
- Prepare yourself by identifying and recapturing a strong positive experience from your past that has the resources you need to handle the upcoming situation.

- Try to place the problem before the both of you, not between the two of you.
- Use framing in front of every communication (including the questions) to give your ex enough context so that she can understand what is being requested or stated. (See p. 178.)
- Use questions plus paraphrasing to understand what she is proposing or saying before responding.
- Talk assertively and speak in terms of how you feel.

Parents' behavior is one of the principle determinants of what children learn, how committed they will become as parents, and what kinds of choices they will make as adults. Children are always studying their mothers and fathers—show them a dad they can be proud of and model for them the best of communication skills. Give your children every opportunity to succeed as parents in the families they create.

Dealing with Your Ex in Court

For you separated or divorced fathers, whether already moved, already dealing with an ex who has moved, contemplating a move, or facing the possibility of a move, it's important to bear in mind that where family law is concerned, Mom and Dad are the key players in the process. You and your ex alone have the power to end your conflicted divorce and move on to an equitable arrangement. When parents manage the process poorly— by relying solely on an attorney's advice, for example—the family pays a high price emotionally and financially. In the many months that preceded the awareness that as parents they have the last word, many divorcing couples choose to hire attorneys.

For a short time lawyers may be an asset. They can explain both legalese and the divorce process itself. Many parents feel reassured standing next to an attorney. The sense of security that some lawyers cultivate becomes a liability when parents forget that for all the years that lie ahead they, not their attorneys, must raise the children.

If one parent generates conflict, the other can ask his or her counsel to bring that fact to the court's attention. For example, a man's attorney might inform the judge that his client would like to return to custody counseling. The judge would most likely honor the request. Once in front of the counselor, a man can demonstrate by a willingness to cooperate that he is the one who wishes to end the dissension, and as we have seen, many counselors will make recommendations to the courts that favor the cooperative parent. If you believe your ex-wife's attorney is interfering with the resolution of the case, you can:

1. Ask the judge to refer both of you to custody counseling
2. Use your own attorney for legal counsel only and represent yourself in court
3. Suggest that your two attorneys use a third attorney as a stand-in judge

When a father tells a member of the judiciary that he wishes to negotiate directly with his ex-wife, it suggests that her attorney is unnecessary. When it appears to the person in charge that the parents are on the verge of working together, there is a good chance he or she will send the couple into custody counseling or mediation. In a counselor's office, the father may be able to convince his ex-wife that the person she hired is a hindrance to their progress and in turn a liability for their children. If his ex-wife disagrees, the father can always return to his own attorney and continue to fight in court.

You could use your attorney for legal counsel only. With a knowledge of how to behave in court and an understanding of procedures, a father could ably present his case. Judges, knowing that parents are the ones who must ultimately raise their children, often prefer to speak directly to Mom and Dad. If the father presents his ideas effectively, and sincerely wants to end the fighting with his ex, the judge may decide the wife's attorney is a hindrance. When that happens, the judge will direct his questions and suggestions to the parents and the lone lawyer is given few opportunities to express himself. Contested divorces tend to be similar; expensive, slow, unimaginative legal contests that keep an attorney's client in ignorance. Mothers and fathers who avoid the stresses of traditional divorces do so by researching fresh solutions. Parents who are open-minded and flexible consider less common means of conflict resolution.

We will address the ins and outs of navigating family court in more detail in a future chapter.

Dealing with Your Ex Outside of Court

Once a father's right to co-parent is recorded in court, his attention must shift to the maintenance of his arrangement. Even if he is unhappy with what the court stipulates, he must still maintain it. Only when he proves he can do what the judge wants him to do will he have a chance to improve his lot. Even those who are delighted with their schedules have to shift their focus; they, too, have to think in terms of the maintenance of their lifestyles if they want the arrangement to last until their child is an adult.

To sustain co-parenting, you, as an engaged father, must make a conscious choice to shift the way you think. In the beginning when you're struggling to establish yourself, you have to think as a chess player might, calculating each move in order to strengthen your own position and limit your ex-wife's moves. Once you have your parenting agreement in hand, you can focus on sustaining your family. By using common sense, practicality, and self-improvement, you can protect your position in the new family structure. Men who work too much or who expose their children to their excessive dating (too many partners, inappropriate actions in front of children, dating too often, and so forth) are sure to trigger negative responses from their ex-wives. (We will deal with each of these problems in greater detail in the next chapter.) If your ex is concerned about the welfare of her children when they are at your house, it is almost certain that you'll both end up back in court. Even men who had cooperative ex-wives from the beginning can fail at co-parenting if they don't make a conscientious effort to parent well. These failures can be doubly painful for men: not only do their families suffer again, but their failures negatively influence judges and that negatively affects other co-parenting cases.

Fathers and the Trap of Self-Isolation

Some men who would like to parent throughout their children's lives will not be allowed to because some mothers will interfere. The ex-husbands of women who are not committed to co-parenting are in a perilous position. If they want to co-parent, they need to do everything within their power to maintain a working relationship with their ex-wives. It is extremely difficult to maintain a relationship with someone who is uncooperative.

The men who succeed reach out to others for support and training. Those who isolate themselves (from their families, children, friends, society in general) generally fail.

During the years it takes for a child to grow into an adult, his or her parents, regardless of the parenting agreement, are sure to disagree intensely at times. Any number of situations can trouble them and in turn stress their relationship. As a result, the parents may at times feel burned out, resentful, or frightened of one another. In any of those states, an ex-wife can be uncooperative. Ex-husbands who are striving to maintain trying relationships under difficult conditions will at times need encouragement. They will also need fresh input in order develop new and better communication skills. Listening to the varied and ever-increasing experiences of other divorced fathers allows men the opportunity to grow in order to deal with their challenges.

Friends also can serve as buffers. For example, when something frightening happens, friends can be the vehicles who help to release emotion. Expressing frustration, fears, and anger to friends often means that ex-husbands do not have to dump their feelings onto their ex-wives. Seldom will ex-wives continue cooperating with those who leave them feeling bad.

Occasionally both parents will be on edge. The simplest situation can lead to an argument. This is especially true when the task at hand is inherently stressful. If parents become lax, the most ordinary events can cause emotions to flare. Ask any kid with divorced parents and you'll get an example.

The Opposite of Isolation: A Long-Distance Communication Success Story

Rick and Ginny have been divorced for over a decade, and their kids, Travis and Tara, are fourteen and twelve, respectively.

The marriage broke up over Rick's drug problem. To make matters worse, while he was in jail on a drug charge, Ginny took the kids and moved out of the area.

Because of Rick's legal problems, he had little leverage where his kids were concerned. He rarely saw them. But once he got out of jail, Rick began trying to put his life back together. As he says in the sidebar that follows, his children were the impetus for turning his life around. He began going to Narcotics Anonymous meetings, and he eventually embraced the twelve-step program. Ginny's candid expression of her own reaction is also quite illuminating.

He Says

"Part of the twelve steps is to make amends to those whom you've wronged. Ginny and I had a lot of baggage, and contact between us had been sporadic for a while. When I got to the part where I had to start making amends to people, I put my kids at the top of that list, because they deserved it, and because without them I would have still been drinking and drugging. I had no idea how I was going to get her to let me talk to them, or even how I was going to get her to hear me out herself. She had taken to hanging up on me, usually after swearing at me. So I talked to my NA (Narcotics Anonymous) sponsor about it. It was a story he had heard before. He put me in touch with several other fathers from my NA group, all of whom had children who lived out of state, and they were all very supportive. When I finally made the call, I got her to listen to me by keeping the discussion focused on the kids. I know that having the support of the guys who had helped me get to that point was a crucial part of it."—Rick, long-distance dad

> **She Says**
>
> "I promised myself when Rick went to jail that his drug problems weren't going to touch our kids as long as I had something to say about it. I'll admit that I was surprised the day he called and told me that he owed us all an 'amends,' and that he wanted to start with the kids. It was quite a beginning. Things aren't perfect by any means, and we still disagree, but they are different, now, and they started to change on that day."—Ginny, Rick's ex-wife

In this situation, results are what you simply *must* keep foremost in mind, because discussing plans with others before taking action will help you avoid decisions that could potentially needlessly alienate your ex-wife. Parents generally seek sole physical and legal custody of a child when they feel insecure or they sense a chance to seize control.

If one adult is isolating but the other is reaching out to friends, the parent who is discussing pertinent issues can often mend an unhappy situation. If parents are not looking for solutions outside of themselves, then their relationship is almost sure to fail. When both parents are searching for tools that will enable them to handle the ongoing challenge of working together, they are almost sure to succeed in maintaining their two homes.

Here are two more reasons why it pays to maintain contact with other long-distance dads who are either "fellow travelers" or "trailblazers" who have experienced much of what you're going through before you have: First, speaking regularly with other divorced fathers helps you remember how and why you got here, and also helps you keep your perspective. Once those old pains are remembered, the reason for checking in with friends becomes as clear as a restraining order—never again do you want to relive the tumultuous time that follows many marital breakups. Without occasional reminders, too, many forgot to remain vigilant, and too often the past is relived. Second, discussing the challenges you have faced with others allows you to know in advance what your children may encounter. And on the other hand, hearing how others have dealt with problems will give you the opportunity to avoid similar mistakes. You may review the discussion on your need for a support network in Chapter 5, "Building a Support Network."

Avoiding Jealousy

Few emotions cause more embarrassment or damage than jealously. After co-parenting on a fifty-fifty basis for eight years, John attended his first support group. In the Divorced Fathers Network meeting, he shared the following:

"I had a great relationship with my ex-wife until I remarried. Immediately after the wedding I was served with papers saying she wanted custody of our children. We live two counties apart, and the next week, when it was time for me to watch them, she refused to bring them to our midway drop-off point. When I phoned her, she told me to get a lawyer. After eight years of cooperation, now she wants full custody. When we went to court, I told the judge I didn't want a custody battle, and I was not going to give up on my kids. He respected me for my attitude and ordered Barbara and I into custody counseling."

Remember that when dealing with your ex, it is in your own best interest to avoid situations where she may feel awkward or ill at ease. Granted, it is not possible to insulate her from every situation that might make her uncomfortable, and that is not a father's job. Still, problems that *can* be avoided *should* be avoided at all costs.

Jealously is likely to get in the way of your attempts to successfully co-parent when one person appears to be replacing the other. I know what you're thinking: isn't that what divorce and remarriage are all about? The answer to that is no. She stopped being your *spouse*; she did not stop being your child's *mother*. This can be as blatant as hearing your daughter talk about how her mother introduced her new boyfriend/husband as the "new daddy," or as indirect as your ex overhearing her children arguing, saying something as silly as, "Daddy's girlfriend loves me more than you. She plays with me more than mommy plays with you." It is important that you and your ex get on the same page about this and then stick to the script once you've written it.

She Says

"Dan, Mickie, and I had a conference about Deirdre's financial aid application for college. We pooled our resources effectively. Dan and Mickie brought their tax returns. I did the filling out of forms because I had recently been a graduate student myself. One of the things that really bothered Dan was that we had to decide for purposes of financial aid who was the custodial parent. The college Deirdre went to had the Divorced Parent's Statement. Dan hated that form because we chose Mickie as the custodial parent and Dan the divorced parent. Mickie made less money, so that heightened Deirdre's eligibility for financial aid. Those were very coldhearted decisions that we made together so Deirdre could attend a very expensive university. That was just one legal area where we ran into a setup where someone's jealously could have been triggered."—Renny, Dan's wife and Dierdre's stepmother.

Strategies for Success

What can a father do to improve communication with counselors, judges, and ex-spouses?

- Show up for appointments on time and pay attention. Listen intently and, as appropriate, repeat back in your own words what you heard him or her say. Remember to ask if what you heard was what the speaker wanted to communicate.
- Make eye contact and show you're listening. Be sure your body language is nonaggressive.
- Put yourself in the position of the other person and try to see the situation from their point of view.
- Use "I" statements to explain what is important to you and avoid blaming the other party. For example, "I'd like to spend more time with the children—I feel it's important to them. I also think when both parents have equal time with the children, there will be less reason for conflict."
- Talk things over with another father—preferably someone also engaged in long-distance parenting—before speaking with counselors, judges, or the children's mother. Ask the other father if you sound angry or blaming. Practice until you can communicate in an assertive, yet nonthreatening manner.
- Say only what is necessary—too much input can confuse the issue.
- Maintain self-control. Sharing children with someone who wants no part of you, or who you want no contact with, requires self-discipline. The better you can communicate, the easier it will be for all those involved.

When parents first separate they often feel angry and defensive. Trust is at an all-time low. There may be a tendency to imagine the worst. One way to short-circuit real or imagined fears is to present all the details that are relevant to the communication at hand.

Importance of Framing

John Grinder, a communications consultant, offered some suggestions to men attending one of our Divorced Fathers Network meetings. *Framing*, he suggested, is a way to give one's former spouse the details and, in turn, the opportunity to fully understand what is being stated or requested.

When she sees the whole picture, she has a better chance of accepting the logic behind any given proposal and the benefits to her.

Framing is the art of first presenting the details that surround one's point or suggestion before discussing the subject itself. Generally, fathers frame statements and questions in order to facilitate cooperation. When a suggestion or idea is well framed, it is easier for the other person(s) to understand and encourages their participation.

Ron, a divorced father, was scheduled for custody mediation in seven days, so he set out to master framing. From one Monday to the next, he made a conscious effort to frame every question and statement that came up in his day-to-day life so it was complete, logical, and appealing. In an average day he'd typically have the opportunity to practice framing fifteen or twenty times. He mastered the fine line between saying too much, and appearing manipulative, and saying too little, and leaving out essential details. His mediation went well: he received more time with his children than he expected. An unforeseen benefit was the kudos he received from his ex-wife, who appreciated the extra details as well as the man's effort to better communicate.

Consider what information you need to provide the other person to further good communication. What relevant information would improve the situation, as opposed to what information would confuse the situation? Just by trying this out you'll see what works and what doesn't. For example, instead of arbitrarily saying to an ex-partner, "I'd like the kids to fly to my house on Friday rather than Saturday," try framing. "I've been thinking that the kids would love to see the educational exhibit on planets at the science museum here. The exhibit closes on Sunday, so I'd like them to arrive on Friday and take them on Saturday. What do you think?"

Now the mother knows why the father wants to change the original plan and have the kids arrive earlier. If she is able to place her children's well-being before any negative feelings she may have, and she, too, feels the kids will benefit from the field trip, the children will arrive on Friday rather than Saturday.

Importance of Asking Specific Questions

Asking specific questions is essential to good communication. These questions allow one to understand exactly what someone else is saying. Often what is heard is not what the speaker intended to communicate. Questions are used to explore what has been said. There are two types that are equally important for good communication: questions that explore consequences and questions that explore a generalization.

First are the questions that explore the *consequences* of what is being presented. For example, one's ex-wife might say, "You are feeding the kids too much junk food when they're with you." Instead of responding defensively—"No I'm not, and stop telling me what to do"—you could pause, take a deep breath, and ask, "What happens when I give the kids junk food?" The mother then has the opportunity to explain the consequences she is trying to avoid. Her explanation could be, "They are so sugared-out after they visit you that when they come back to my house, they don't fall asleep until after midnight, and their schoolwork suffers because I have to send them to school tired."

People are surprised at how often exploring the consequences of the subject at hand leads to a better understanding and, in turn, works to the benefit of both parents and children. An added benefit is that a full disclosure allows the mother to feel heard and, as a result, more willing to communicate with you. In such instances, questioning can lead to a better co-parenting relationship—the father more thoroughly understands the problem, and the mother is pleased by his willingness to get to the core of their issues.

Sometimes, though, an ex-spouse's answer will make absolutely no sense. When that happens, you can simply say, "I'm sorry. I'm not sure I understand," and instead request, "Can you clarify . . . can you tell me more about your concerns?" Questions are also helpful when you want to explore a generalization. Accepting a broad statement, especially if it is accusatory, often means a missed opportunity to research the issue at hand. For example: If his ex-wife were to say, "Joe, you don't know how to take care of little children," Joe might respond, "Tell me specifically what makes you think I can't take care of our children." His ex's answer could clarify for Joe exactly what her concerns are, such as Joe's never having toddler-proofed his new home or his not knowing how to put their child to sleep because he had never been around to do it before.

Asking questions can also bring insight into what the other person intends to communicate later on. With that information, one can better prepare for what is to come.

Communicating Effectively

If a father wishes to communicate as effectively as possible, he needs to examine the issue(s) at hand and to do so from a variety of perspectives. The more perspectives a father has, the better his chances of finding a fresh solution. Too often, men see a conflict exclusively from their point of view. Some, however, will consider their ex-wife's vantage point, and it is these individuals who have a better chance of resolving conflict than those who are narrow-minded. Understanding another person's take on a problem doesn't necessarily mean that you agree with it.

Communicating Through E-Mail

We've already talked quite a bit about both the importance of communication and the ways that we can use technology to help facilitate it. Let's take a moment to talk about some of the potential unintended consequences of e-mail communication.

While it's easy to keep e-mail correspondence as a record of what you have discussed, e-mail communication itself is not without potential for peril. For example, e-mail is written correspondence, and there is a wide degree of latitude in how the reader can gauge "tone" in an e-mail, especially if either correspondent is prone to sarcasm. This can lead to potential misunderstanding, and we all know where that can lead.

How to combat this? Simple. E-mail is a terrific tool when used responsibly. It's a wonderful means to nail down things discussed in more free-flowing verbal conversations via either the phone or the Web.

For example, it's very effective when you begin an e-mail thusly: *"Barbara, to summarize our phone discussion of today, Monday, July 22, as I understand it, I've agreed to purchase Sarah's plane ticket for her return flight to Florida after spending the rest of the summer here in Ohio with me, and you have agreed that we will split the cost of her travel back and forth between our two homes from now on. Did I get this right? Let me know what you think.—Jim."* Whether Barbara responds and you fine-tune your understanding of this conversation is really immaterial. You're documenting your conversations, and if she allows your e-mail to go unanswered, in places like family court, the rule of thumb is that "silence implies consent." Either way, you are definitely covered.

When used correctly, e-mail can be a powerful communication tool. Make sure that you keep it just that!

Stepparents and Their Role in Communicating with Your Children's Mother

One potential pitfall for long-distance parents is answering the question of where their new spouse fits into the existing long-distance parenting paradigm. After all, we've just established that you don't want to upset the applecart once you've got things all sorted out.

One frequent mistake long-distance parents make here is to place a stepparent in the position of mediator; the divorced couple converse via this "neutral" person. There are major problems with using stepparents as go-betweens.

You would think that intelligent, rational (in theory) people would realize that doing something like this is not only unwise, but it is abdicating much of the responsibility in which you justifiably take so much pride when it comes to parenting your kids. And yet it happens all the time. No matter how you may feel about your ex *personally*, this is in many ways a business relationship, and unless you are interested in paying the potential price

YOUR KIDS' MOM: YOUR ALLY IN PARENTING

(both fiscally and emotionally where your kids are concerned) of alienating your ex on this, you should never do it.

Here's a great example of why:

Gail has been struggling in her co-parenting relationship with Les for nine years. He married his second wife, Alise, six years ago. She became the stepmother to Marisa and trouble began. Gail recalls it starting this way:

"One afternoon, Alise came up to me and said Les told her to handle the visitation scheduling. Les hadn't said one word to me beforehand. I was so angry and humiliated. Alise told me that from now on, there would be only one phone number I could call to speak with Les. I was to leave a message on his answering machine, and after they had talked, Alise would get back to me. I wanted to be able to talk directly to Les about Marisa's school. Some things you have to discuss and process. Like how are we going to handle her homework or drama classes? Co-parenting can't be done on an answering machine. And it got weirder. After that Alise said to me, 'Gail, you have to be good to me because I'm the only one who will talk with you.' That statement filled me with anxiety. I won't communicate with him through his new wife anymore. I sent them a letter requesting private mediation. If they don't agree to voluntary mediation, I'll get court-ordered mediation and Alise won't be allowed in, because only parents can talk in there." As a long-distance dad, you should know that wherever the kids are the majority of the time is where the mediation will most likely be. However, if you are in good communication with your ex-wife, you can generally work out an arrangement that is convenient for both parties.

Now, imagine that the tables are turned in the above story genderwise. Imagine it's you and your ex we're discussing in this example, and she has remarried, and all of a sudden she refuses to speak to you, and insists that you speak only with her new husband. Would you take that lying down?

Of course not; you would do something about it. This is where that old mantra of "respect, respect, respect" comes into play (yet again). Imagine if Les had the great good sense to simply follow the Golden Rule and treat his ex as he wished to be treated? Do you think that Les would like it if the shoe were on the other foot?

There is another side to this story, and Les probably thinks he's completely justified in taking this extreme approach, perhaps because he considers Gail difficult to work with. After all, people get divorced for reasons, and usually good ones.

The Benefits

In the end, if nothing else sways you on this, look at it as a simple equation. Acting like an adult and sucking it up and working *with* your ex (no matter how difficult she can be) on this sort of thing is going to get you:

- More time with your kids
- Less paid out in child support
- Less stress on your kids
- Less spent on attorneys' fees
- Less money spent flying back and forth in order to go to court each time an argument happens

On the other hand, if you don't mind paying child support and spending a ton of your time in family court, and you think your divorce lawyer is underpaid, then have at it, take this tack. Just remember that actions have consequences!

The willingness to communicate (there's that word again, at least as important as "respect") is what maintains long-distance parenting. Without continued dialogue between fathers and mothers, there is little chance of ever creating mutual respect. One of the biggest benefits of long-distance parenting to children is the advantage of living in two homes with parents who have earned the admiration of each other.

This is not to say that if and when you and your ex remarry that the stepparents don't have a role to play in the family structure. There are many "blended" families out there where stepparents are recognized as having a place in the family. How much say your new spouse (or your ex's new spouse, for that matter) has regarding the supervision of your child within the family structure is something that you and your ex (and only you two, perhaps with the aid of a family counselor) will need to work out together. Fail to work it out together now, and you run the risk of needing a family court judge to act as referee and work it out for you.

In the end, it's obviously important that you get along with your ex. If you can honestly become friends in the course of establishing a strong long-distance parenting partnership, so much the better. However, being "friends" isn't really required. What is required is respect, patience, and a willingness to observe the Golden Rule of treating that other person the way you yourself would like to be treated.

Establishing a solid relationship with your child's mother will not only pay direct dividends for you, but it'll take a lot of the strain off of your kids. And really, in the end, isn't this all about making things easier for them?

13

Dating as a Divorced, Long-Distance Dad

"To fear love is to fear life, and those who fear life are already three parts dead."
—Lord Russell (1872–1970)

DATING WHILE HELPING RAISE ONE'S KIDS FROM a distance is a common thing in this age of divorce. Once you have grieved over the loss of your marriage, it will be natural for you to want to date again. If you approach it correctly, dating while co-parenting need not be troublesome. Seeking companionship or romance is not a problem for long-distance parents when done responsibly. Ideally, divorced parents will discuss, before either begins the search for a new partner, how to handle the introduction of new people into the family. Fears can be managed by talking in advance about limiting the children's exposure to their parents' love interests. Such a discussion is personally challenging, and timing is important. For example, it would be foolish to discuss dating with a former lover who still hurts from being abandoned.

Talk It Over with Your Ex First

To some fathers the idea of discussing future dating with their children's mother is scary. They think things like, "What if she freaks out, gets jealous or hateful, and takes me to court? She could take my children away from me." It is certainly wise to consider how the children's mother might react.

At the same time, it is best if fear does not stand in the way of necessary discussion. A well-thought-out talk can do much to eliminate the potential for conflict. One way to lessen the impact and to demonstrate respect is to make the announcement in a short letter. Correspondence affords the parents the opportunity to communicate early in the dating process. Furthermore, writing your thoughts down *before* you broach the subject of dating in a face-to-face conversation with your ex will force you to organize your thoughts and can make it easier for you both to discuss your feelings and air your potential concerns. A note of intent can be both a demonstration of respect for the former spouse's feelings and a testament to your commitment to shared parenting.

An example might look something like this:

> *Hello Katherine,*
> *I hope all is well with you. Things are fine on this end, still committed to working with you to raise the best of children.*
> *Can we discuss a matter that is important to me? I want to find a companion and plan to start dating soon. Rest assured this will be a slow and responsible process. The children will not be introduced to a string of acquaintances. As you know, in their eyes you are the best mother in the world. I reinforce that at every opportunity.*

After considering their feelings and after much introspection, I believe I can date without disturbing them. All dating will occur when the kids are with you, and there will be no overnight visitors when the children are at my home. Anyone I find interesting will be screened to eliminate those who may be incapable of fitting into our family. If I find someone who I believe may fit, you and the kids will meet her. How you feel about a potential companion of mine matters. If you have a concern about anyone I spend time with, please share your thoughts with me. Feel free to respond with a letter.

Regards, Brett

Again, honest and considerate correspondence helps to demonstrate your respect for your ex-wife's feelings and your intention to protect the emotions of those in the family. After all, just because you're no longer married doesn't mean you're supposed to stop respecting each other. As we discussed in our chapter about successfully communicating with your ex (and as we have revisited this concept over and over again throughout this book), the marriage might be over, but your relationship with your children pretty much ensures that you're going to need to continue to have one with your ex, and the most successful ones, the ones where everyone gets what they need out of the situation, are relationships based first, last, and always on *respect.*

Opportunities to Date

Ambitious men have ample opportunity to date. Well-thought-out shared parenting does not limit people; instead it allows for fuller lives. Dads can go dancing or to the movies when the kids are secure with their mothers (and the reverse is equally true). The opportunity for single people to raise children, work, and play is another advantage to co-parenting. It is easy to parent one week and date the next. For most single fathers dating is not a problem, but there are certain rules that it's in your best interest to both keep in mind and rigorously observe.

Let's look at a couple of examples of what many dating dads do when they first get back into the dating game. The first will be a good example of what *not* to do. The second will be an example of a father who successfully navigated the rocks and shoals of dating.

What Not to Do

Chris, divorced for two years from Courtney, and father of five-year-old Stephen, recalls what it felt like to get back into the dating scene: "I felt like I'd gotten paroled. New job, new city, new life. I paid my monthly check and felt like I was doing my part. I had plenty of resources left over, so I went to the clubs, met lots of gals eager to get to know me better. We'd have some laughs, go out a few times, and then, if things started to get serious, I'd hit them with the fact that I have a kid on the other coast. Now, I'm thirty, and most of these gals were just that: 'gals,' not much over twenty-one, and the idea of an insta-family really cooled most of their jets. Next thing I knew, I was wondering why I couldn't meet the kind of woman I would actually like to introduce to my kid."

What to Do

Matthew, who separated from his wife, Nikki, when their daughter Jennifer was six, took a different approach to dating once he felt he was ready. "Nikki and I married in our late twenties, and by the time I was ready to start dating again, I was thirty-three. I promised myself that I wouldn't date until my divorce had been final for a year. While I was busy getting my life together, Jennifer and I talked a lot about me dating. By then she was eight (going on eighteen!), and was very curious about what it would be like to have a stepmother. By the time I started looking around to date again, she was trying to set me up with her teacher!"

When to Date

It is important that during the first year both parents date only when the children are at the other home. Men who invite dates over too soon after their divorce are being insensitive to their kid's feelings. Again, divorce can be devastating for children as well as for their parents, and also again, the answer to the question of how best to address this concern is demonstrate respect; not just for your ex, but for your children as well. It's not something you can fake, and it's not something with which you can (or should) barter. It is a necessity that you demonstrate wherever and whenever and with whomever it is appropriate during those first difficult days after your divorce.

Children can be extremely loyal to their parents and to their past marriage. Sometimes, years after the divorce, kids still hope Mom and Dad will get back together.

One father, Raymond, a commercial refrigeration contractor, had this experience: "Eight months after my divorce I walked into my bedroom and found Jessie, my five-year-old, standing on my dresser trying with all his might to rehang his mother's and my wedding picture. He was crying. It broke my heart seeing him try to rehang the picture of his mom and dad."

When new people are introduced into a child's life, they may not be welcomed; at least not at first. Many parents do not realize that for their kids, no one can ever take the place of the other parent. While replacing his children's mother may not have been the father's intention, the presence of another woman is often enough to trigger both a child's sense of loyalty toward their mother and a streak of defiance toward their father. After all, dads cannot simply force their children to accept someone new into their hearts. You can save yourself, your children, and your new friends a great deal of embarrassment by going slow.

Some Points to Consider When Dating Again

Dating a single parent is more complicated than going out with someone who does not have children and an ex-wife (i.e., *you*). Patience and caution will pay off. Here are a few points to consider when dating:

- Many women without children of their own do not understand how challenging it is to date men with children. It could well take them months to fully comprehend the dynamics necessary to fit into the family. Dealing with a combative ex-wife and/or hostile stepchildren is reason enough for many girlfriends to leave a relationship.
- Few women (again we're speaking about those without children of their own) are prepared for the realization that the children's needs come before their own. Girlfriends often come and go, but a conscientious father's number-one commitment is (and ought to be) to his kids. This kind of simple truth can often be difficult for people without children of their own to accept.

- It takes many women in this sort of situation a year or more to discover whether or not they are capable of stepparenting throughout the child's life. It will take vast amounts of patience on your part to allow the new woman in your life to decide if shared parenting works for her.

And now, from the man's perspective. Here's where an ounce of prevention is worth a pound of cure. Fathers should be patient when dating because:

- Since children should be Dad's first priority, and raising kids is time-consuming, it will take a father longer to move through the dating process than it does a man without kids. Fathers simply have fewer hours to spend with the women of their dreams than bachelors do.
- Single dads tend to be busy people and many discover after dating awhile that "working on their relationship" is not high enough on their list of priorities to satisfy a girlfriend—children simply must come first.
- Some discover that spending time with kids is simpler and more fun than dating. This is especially true in relationships with women who need large blocks of "quality time" with their mate in order to feel loved.
- Fathers who believe a casual relationship with a woman will lessen their parenting load are mistaken. Parenting time and responsibilities increase as children age, and the older kids are, the more they want to do. Ask the guardian of a fourteen-year-old how much time he or she has for dating, and the answer will probably be "little or none."

Danny has a ten-year-old daughter and a son who is twelve. He says, "Most of the women I date already know about my family. If not, I tell them right off. The conversation goes like this: 'I'm a single dad with two kids. If you and I have a relationship, you have one with my kids, too. We're a package with a lot to offer.' I'll be jovial when talking to her about a possible relationship between her and me, but I'll make sure she understands I am completely committed to my kids. If she is mature she'll respect me for having that attitude and accept the limits my devotion to my family places on her relationship with me."

Time can be generous. It affords you the opportunity to establish the fact that your girlfriend can make a positive contribution to your children's lives. If she is not a good role model for their education, career, or relationships, your children need to be shielded from her so they do not have the opportunity to become emotionally attached.

Referring back to stepmother Renny as an example: "I believe that all parenting is elective. When I got to know Deirdre, I wanted a relationship with her. Whether you're biologically related to your child or not, you choose whether you want to parent a child."

Questions to Ask Your Date and Yourself

Here are some practical questions you as a single father should always ask when you start dating someone:

- Does she want to have children of her own? If she does, will that work with your plans for the future?
- Is she financially self-sufficient? Most single fathers have a finite amount of income; if they do, the children deserve the lion's share.

- Does she want to help with the parenting? If not, this could be a flashpoint down the road.
- Was she abused as a child? Not all abused children grow up to be abusers, but some do. If she was abused and she's around your children, her past could manifest itself and your family will have to deal with her issues. Fathers have every right to ask, with respect and kindness, about their prospective mate's past.

It is equally important that fathers ask themselves questions, such as:

- Do I want to marry again? If not, the woman needs to be told immediately before she or the children are emotionally hurt.
- Am I only physically attracted to this person? Children can (and should) be shielded from relationships that will end when the lust dies down.
- Am I placing my family's well-being before my desire to find a companion? If not, can I expect my co-parenting to last?
- Do I have any issues such as emotional difficulties, sexual or physical abuse, or substance abuse problems that need to be addressed before attempting another relationship?
- Do I have reason to expect my next relationship to be better than my past marriage? People who have divorced should, when the time is right, get some counseling to determine why the last marriage did not work, to examine their role in the breakup, and to ask what they have done so the next serious relationship does not hit the same barrier.

Asking these questions will lead you on the road to finding a healthy relationship that you, and your children, can enjoy.

Boundaries

Children with divorced parents are in a precarious position. If both mom and dad are dating, the odds are high that children's hearts will again be broken by a loved one leaving.

Of course there are no guarantees that a relationship will last—a truth that children with divorced parents learn quickly. Because of the sense of loss that kids feel when loved ones leave their life, it is ludicrous to ask them to accept more than a few women into their families. If the father wants to be respected as a parent, he needs to do everything within his power to be sure that the people he invites into the family have a sincere desire to remain. The more selective you are, the less risk there is for your children that they will lose a woman they have learned to love.

The fact that children can bond quickly with other people can create problems. Generally it takes adults longer to commit to each other than it does for kids to open their hearts to strangers. After only a few meetings with an acquaintance, children can be asking, "Daddy, is Susan your girlfriend? Can she stay for dinner? Can she sleep over?" One way to temper the children's enthusiasm is to remind them that Susan is a friend who has her own home and life to look after. Fathers can refer to prospective mates as friends until they feel certain both adults are committed and that their relationship will be long-lived. However, children are immediately going to start speculating on the significance of this dating relationship, even if it amounts to just going out to have coffee. So it is best to tell them as honestly as is age-appropriate and keep them informed as the dynamics of the relationship change. Do not say anything to a child that you don't want voiced at the most inopportune time.

Just the opposite can happen as well, though. Children four or older are apt to dislike the idea of Dad getting involved in a serious relationship, at least initially. To bridge this gap, if the relationship is turning serious, plan activities that give the child or children a chance to play with and have fun with the new prospective person in their lives. Little things like playing catch, shooting baskets, and going rollerblading are good activities— as is anything else that is fun and noncompetitive.

As a friend, when she visits she's welcome to socialize. Hopefully everyone will interact and enjoy each other's company. As the family grows accustomed to her, the two of you should begin to discuss boundaries. For instance, her relationship with you will be best served if:

- She aligns herself with you, the father (at least publicly), thus supporting your position as the primary parent.
- She avoids publicly taking the children's side in arguments and never debates with you in front of your kids. If she attempts to get acceptance from the children by supporting their cause, she jeopardizes her relationship with you, as well as your relationship with your children, by undermining your authority over them.
- She relates to the children as an adult to a child, never as their peer. If her relationship with you moves past dating, she will want the children to treat her as an adult, not as a "pal."

When You're Uncomfortable with Who Your Child's Mother Dates

Remember how we've talked about your operating from a position of respect in situations that arise over the course of establishing a co-parenting plan with your ex? Well, here's a situation guaranteed to be ticklish at best and ugly at worst, especially if you don't remember to be respectful of your ex and her feelings while dealing with it. We're talking about intervening in your ex's relationship with someone when that relationship is adversely affecting your children.

Think about it: would you welcome such an intrusion? Not likely! So the question is how do you go about "intruding" in a positive and respectful manner when confronted with this sort of dilemma?

It's probably best to bear in mind that fathers have the right to look out for their children's feelings even when the kids are at Mom's house. All of the screening and boundaries that fathers practice ought to apply equally to their ex-wives as well. Mothers, too, must practice discretion when dating.

When inappropriate forms of adult play at mom's house come to light, they need to be addressed immediately. The most common unacceptable practice in this situation is the mother sleeping with a new boyfriend while the kids are home, especially during the first year. Most judges frown on this. They know that parents sleeping with people other than the kid's biological parent is upsetting and can emotionally damage children when they're still adjusting to the reality of the divorce. This issue should be addressed during the initial efforts to lay the groundwork to continue being good parents. Assuming you are in good communication with your ex-wife, ask, "How are we going to handle dating and intimacy with others, when that time happens?" Here, Dad can help Mom and vice-versa. "When that time comes, send me the kids for a day or two, or let's let them go stay with Grandmother or their aunt."

If you become aware that your ex-wife's relationship with her new boyfriend is emotionally hurting your kids, you need to do something about it. Most men do feel afraid. They will not want to upset the ex-wife. Most children experience some measure of emotional disruption when the family dynamics change, so it's possible that there is nothing unusual happening. However, pay attention to your intuition. If you have a feeling something is wrong, check it out. Investigate further.

If Dad has reason to believe that Mom's boyfriend is involved in drug use, drug distribution, drug manufacturing, physical abuse, child neglect, or anything else equally as serious, he is best advised to notify either law enforcement or social services. Social services will make a home visit or possibly go to the school to interview the child. If they find reason for concern, action will be taken. Any parent with custodial rights will be notified.

Most men do eventually take action, usually in spite of this understandable fear. Allowing unhealthy situations to fester unchecked can create more resentment than immediately addressing poor behavior. The ex-wife might at first be angry, but eventually she may respect you for having the courage to refuse to ignore a potentially problematic situation. Of course, as a father, you must always practice good judgment when confronting your ex with her behavior.

Within the first year an ex-husband can often persuade his ex-wife to stop sleeping with lovers in her home when the kids are there. A respectful letter stating his concern that their children will be emotionally hurt might do the trick. If that does not work, a man can bring his ex-wife's behavior to the attention of their court-appointed psychologist, custody counselor, or judge. It is almost certain that an inappropriately sexually active ex-wife will receive official direction to cool her libido until the children are at Dad's house.

Sometimes the insistence of a father that his former spouse curtail her dating when their children are present works to increase his time with the kids. For example, when a divorced woman has her children every day of the month except for two weekends, she soon realizes that the schedule limits her sex life. If she is approached by the father in a considerate manner with an offer to watch the children when she wants to date, she may accept the father's offer to watch their children. If this works out, in a few months, when the timing feels right, the father may negotiate a change in the parenting schedule.

CONCLUSION

Fathers Forever

OBVIOUSLY, I HAVE THROWN A LOT OF IDEAS AT YOU IN THIS BOOK.
If I've given you only *one* thing to think about, one way in which
to positively impact your relationship with the children from
whom you are separated (either often or sporadically) by distance, then you've gotten your money's worth. At the very least
I've given you plenty to think about.

I wrote this book because I believe passionately that children are meant by both biology and by Providence to have two
parents, and that a father is (and ought to be) more than just
someone the kids see every other weekend and who sends Mom
a check every month. But that's only half the equation.

Over the past decade, I have seen the toll that physical separation takes not just on the children of divorce and on the single
parents who are coping with their new situation, but also on the
families of road-warrior dads, deployed dads, and other fathers
whose circumstances force them to be absent from daily family
life for extended periods of time. I have sat with newly separated fathers who have tearfully poured out their hearts about
how devastated they are by the experience of breaking up their
marital home and playing a diminished role in the lives of their
children. I have interviewed military men who have done multiple tours overseas in both Afghanistan and Iraq, and have

discussed life situations with men who spend half of their calendar year traveling for work. I have talked with these men, counseled them, and advocated tirelessly on their behalf, because I don't want to see them fail as fathers.

No one wants that. If you're divorced, and you and your ex have hard feelings toward each other, remember that those feelings will fade with a combination of time and the change in your living situation, and eventually, most of the mothers of our children will also realize that their kids (and ours) need a father figure in their collective lives. If you're not divorced but are away from your family for significant amounts of time due to work, then go out of your way to be kind to your spouse, because she's carrying the water for multiple people here and deserves some recognition.

In the end, though, it's really about our kids. As fathers, we remember the day our kids were born, what it was like when they took their first steps, the first time they said "Da-da," and how that tiny hand felt wrapped around our fingers when they were still sleeping in their cribs. How could we, as responsible, caring, committed human beings, with a heart, a brain, and a soul, not want what is absolutely the best of all possible worlds for these, the most important things in our lives?

So here's wishing you success in your quest to be an effective father, whether you're divorced, a road warrior, a deployed dad, or some combination of the above. Remember that it begins and ends with respect: respect for your kids, respect for their mother, and, above all, respect for yourself. After all, if you succeed, your kids are the ones who will reap the majority of the benefits.

And what father wouldn't want that outcome?

Suggested Reading and Additional Resources

Books

Ashley, Steve A. *Starting a Divorced Fathers Network.* Santa Cruz, California: Divorced Fathers Network, 2000.

Biller, Henry B. *Fathers and Families: Paternal Factors in Child Development.* Westport, Connecticut: Auburn House, 1993.

Blau, Melinda. *Families Apart: Ten Keys to Successful Co-parenting.* New York: Putnam, 1993.

Braver, Sanford L., and Diane O'Connell. *Divorced Dads: Shattering the Myths.* New York: Putnam, 1998.

Condrell, Kenneth N., and Linda L. Small. *Be a Great Divorced Dad.* New York: St. Martin's Press, 1998.

Farrell, Warren. *The Best Interests of the Child.* DVD, 2006.

Farrell, Warren. *Father and Child Reunion: How to Bring the Dads We Need to the Children We Love.* New York: Putnam, 2001.

Gardner, Richard A. *The Boys and Girls Book About Divorce.* Northvale, New Jersey: Bantam, 1970.

Garrity, Carla B., and Mitchell A. Baris. *Caught in the Middle; Protecting the Children of High-Conflict Divorce.* New York: Lexington Books, 1994.

Gitchel, Sam, and Lorri Foster. *Let's Talk About S-E-X—A Guide for Kids 9 to 12 and Their Parents.* Minnetonka, Minnesota: Book Peddlers, Inc., 1983.

Gough, Michael. *The Virtual Visitation Handbook—A Guide to Personal Video Conferencing.* Copyright © 2004–2006 internet visitation.org

Haltzman, Scott. *The Secrets of Happily Married Men—Eight Ways to Win Your Wife's Heart Forever.* San Francisco: Jossey-Bass, 2007.

Hewitt, Doug. *The Practical Guide to Weekend Parenting.* Long Island City, New York: Hatherleigh Press, 2006.

Johnson, Spencer. *The One Minute Father.* New York: Morrow, 1983.

Klatte, William C. *Live-Away Dads: Staying a Part of Your Children's Lives When They Aren't a Part of Your Home.* New York: Penguin, 1999.

Knox, David. *The Divorced Dad's Survival Book: How to Stay Connected With Your Kids.* New York: Perseus, 2000.

Leving, Jeffery M. *Fathers' Rights—Hard-Hitting and Fair Advice for Every Father Involved in a Custody Battle.* New York: Basic Books, 1998.

Mackey, Wade C. *The American Father: Biocultural and Developmental Aspects.* New York: Plenum, 1996.

Mandelstein, Paul. *Always Dad: Being a Great Father During and After Divorce.* Berkeley: NOLO, 2006.

Marcus, David L. *What It Takes to Pull Me Through—Why Teenagers Get in Trouble and How Four of Them Got Out.* Boston: Houghton Mifflin, 2006.

Meeker, Meg. *Strong Fathers, Strong Daughters—10 Secrets Every Father Should Know.* New York: Ballantine Books, 2007.

The National Fatherhood Initiative. *Deployed Fathers and Families: Deployment Guide for Military Personnel.* New York: FatherSource.org, 2003.

The National Fatherhood Initiative. *Father Facts.* New York: FatherSource.org, 2007.

The National Institute for Building Long-Distance Relationships. *Dads at a Distance: An Activities Handbook For Strengthening Long Distance Relationships.* New York: A & E Family Publishers, 2001.

Nielsen, Linda. *Embracing Your Father—How to Build the Relationship You've Always Wanted with Your Dad.* New York: McGraw-Hill, 2004.

Panatera, Annetta L. *Dad's Time Tracker—Get More Time With Your Children and Manage Your Child Support.* Marietta, Georgia: Kindred Souls Press, 2005.

Panatera, Annetta L. *Mom's Time Tracker—Organize Your Busy Schedule and Safeguard Your Children's Way of Life.* Marietta, Georgia: Kindred Souls Press, 2006.

Parks, Steve. *Teach Me Daddy.* Burleson, Texas: Poetry Pals, 2004.

Ricci, Isolina. *Mom's House, Dad's House; Making Two Homes for Your Child.* New York: A Fireside Book, Simon & Schuster, 1997.

Shimberg, Elaine Fantle, and Michael Shimberg. *The Complete Single Father.* Avon, Massachusetts: Adams Media, 2007.

Winchester, Kent, and Roberta Beyer. *What in the World Do You Do When Your Parents Divorce—A Survival Guide for Kids.* Minneapolis: Free Spirit Publishing, 2001.

Web Sites

American Association for Marriage and Family Therapy
www.aamft.org/index_nm.asp

American Coalition for Fathers and Children
www.acfc.org

The American Red Cross
http://redcross.org

Center for Successful Fathering
www.fathering.org

Dads and Daughters
www.dadsanddaughters.org

Divorce, Custody, Child Support, and Other Resources for
Single Fathers
www.dadsrights.org

The Divorced Fathers Network
www.divorcedfathers.com

Divorce Headquarters
www.divorcehq.com

Divorce Recovery Support Groups
www.divorcecare.org

Divorce Source
www.divorcesource.com

Divorce Wizards
www.divorcewizards.com

Fathers and Families
www.fathersandfamilies.org/site/index.php

The Fatherhood Coalition
www.fatherhoodcoalition.org

The Fathers' Network
www.fathersnetwork.org

The Military Child Education Coalition
http://militarychild.org

Military OneSource
www.militaryonesource.com

National Center for Fathering
www.fathers.com

National Fatherhood Initiative
www.fatherhood.org

Operation: Military Kids
http://operationmilitarykids.org

Parents Without Partners
www.parentswithoutpartners.com

The Salvation Army
www.salvationarmyusa.org

St. Vincent DePaul
http://svdpusa.org

Veterans Affairs Kids Page
www.va.gov/kids

Predeployment Contingency Forms

FORM 1. IMPORTANT FINANCIAL INFORMATION

CHECKING ACCOUNT

Account number	
Type of checking	
Bank name	
Address	
Phone	

SAVINGS ACCOUNT

Account number	
Type of savings	
Bank name	
Address	
Phone	
Savings goal	

MONEY MARKET ACCOUNT

Account number	
Bank name	
Address	
Phone	

CERTIFICATES OF DEPOSIT

Certificate numbers	
Location of certificate	
Maturity date	
What to do when certificate matures	

CREDIT UNION

Account number	
Bank name	
Address	
Phone	

SAFE-DEPOSIT BOX NUMBER

Key is located at	
Contents	

FORM 1. IMPORTANT FINANCIAL INFORMATION *(continued)*

STOCKS AND BONDS

Company name and phone number	
What to do when bond matures	
Company name and phone number	
What to do when bond matures	

LIFE INSURANCE

Life insurance policy number	
Carrier	
Agent name, address, and phone	
Location of papers	
Beneficiary	
Monthly payment	
Automatic deduction	❏ YES ❏ NO

CAR INSURANCE

Car insurance policy number	
Carrier	
Agent name, address, and phone	
Location of papers	
Expiration date	
Monthly payment	
Automatic deduction	❏ YES ❏ NO

HOME OWNER'S INSURANCE

Home owner's insurance policy number	
Carrier	
Agent name, address, and phone	
Location of papers	
Expiration date	
Monthly payment	
Automatic deduction	❏ YES ❏ NO

FORM 2. IMPORTANT MEDICAL INFORMATION

HEALTH INSURANCE

Health insurance policy number	
Carrier	
Agent name, address, and phone	
Location of health insurance cards	
Expiration date	
Monthly payment	
Automatic deduction	❑ YES ❑ NO

DENTAL INSURANCE

Dental insurance policy number	
Carrier	
Agent name, address, and phone	
Location of dental insurance cards	
Expiration date	
Monthly payment	
Automatic deduction	❑ YES ❑ NO

PRESCRIPTION PLAN

Prescription plan number	
Carrier	
Agent name, address, and phone	
Location of prescription cards	
Expiration date	
Monthly payment	
Automatic deduction	❑ YES ❑ NO

PRIMARY CARE PHYSICIAN

Name	
Address	
Phone	

PEDIATRICIAN

Name	
Address	
Phone	

FORM 2. IMPORTANT MEDICAL INFORMATION *(continued)*

HOSPITAL

Name	
Address	
Phone	

DENTIST

Name	
Address	
Phone	

PHARMACY

Name	
Address	
Phone	
Emergency information	

DAD

Allergic to	
Blood type	

MOM

Allergic to	
Blood type	

CHILDREN

Name	
Allergic to	
Blood type	
Location of shot records	
Name	
Allergic to	
Blood type	
Location of shot records	

FORM 3. HELPFUL PHONE NUMBERS

Mom's work	
Next-door neighbor	
In-laws	
Primary care	
Family doctor	
Pediatrician	
Supervisors	
Babysitter	
School	
Mechanic	
Tow truck	
Friend	
Friend	
Friend	
Plumber	
Cable	
Bank	
Mortgage	
Auto insurance	
Base/post commander's office	
Pizza	

FORM 4. IMPORTANT INFORMATION ABOUT FAMILY MEMBERS

DAD	
Dad's name	
Rank	
Social Security number	
Unit identification	
APO number	
Birth date	
DEPENDENTS	
Mom's name	
Social Security number	
Employer	
Birth date	
CHILDREN	
Name	
Birth date	
Social Security number	
Current grade	
School name	
Name	
Birth date	
Social Security number	
Current grade	
School name	
HIS PARENTS'	
Names	
Addresses	
Phone numbers	
HER PARENTS'	
Names	
Addresses	
Phone numbers	
CLOSEST RELATIVE	
Name	
Number	

FORM 5. IMPORTANT INFORMATION ABOUT PET CARE

VETERINARIAN

Name	
Address	
Phone	

PETS

Pet's name	
Rabies shot due	
Yearly shots due	
Registration papers location	
Special instructions	
Pet's name	
Rabies shot due	
Yearly shots due	
Registration papers location	
Special instructions	
Pet's name	
Rabies shot due	
Yearly shots due	
Registration papers location	
Special instructions	
Pet's name	
Rabies shot due	
Yearly shots due	
Registration papers location	
Special instructions	
Pet's name	
Rabies shot due	
Yearly shots due	
Registration papers location	
Special instructions	

FORM 6. IMPORTANT PAPERS AND PROCEDURES

WILL

Will	❑ YES ❑ NO
Location	
Living will	❑ YES ❑ NO
Location	

ORGAN DONORS

Is anyone an organ donor?	❑ YES ❑ NO
Name	
Noted on driver's license	❑ YES ❑ NO
Name	
Noted on driver's license	❑ YES ❑ NO

POWER OF ATTORNEY

Power of Attorney	❑ YES ❑ NO
For parents or others	❑ YES ❑ NO
Attorney	

BIRTH CERTIFICATES

Name	
Location	
Name	
Location	
Name	
Location	
Name	
Location	

MARRIAGE CERTIFICATES

Location	

BURIAL PROCEDURES

Husband	
Wife	
Children	

FORM 7. RESOURCES FOR HOME ISSUES

PHONE NUMBERS

Plumbing	
Electrical	
Appliances	
Heat, oil/gas	
Phone company	
Computer	
Air conditioner	
Garbage removal	
Snow removal	
Lawn service/mower repair	
Security system	

WHAT TO DO IF YOU HAVE

No water	
To prime the pump	
No electric	
To replace fuses/set circuit breakers	
No gas	
No heat	
No phone	
To shut off water	
Main shut-off valve location	

LOCATION OF KEYS AND SECURITY INFORMATION

House key	
Car key	
Padlock combination	
Storage key	
Other keys	
Safe-deposit box	
Lock box	

FORM 7. RESOURCES FOR HOME ISSUES *(continued)*

AUTO INFORMATION

Local mechanic	
Name	
Address	
Phone	
Local garage covers repairs for	
Towing company	
Name	
Address	
Phone	
Car or travel club	
Address	
Phone	
Car	
Make	
Model	
Year	
Tag number	
Inspection due	
Take to	
Car	
Make	
Model	
Year	
Tag number	
Inspection due	
Take to	

Family Law

The Twofold Path of Argument:
The first path is learning the tools and moves;
The second path is concentration and relaxation.
One without the other does not work.
—Michael A. Gilbert,
How to WIN an Argument

FAMILY-LAW COURTS PREFER RECORDING PARENTING AGREEMENTS to ordering them. In most cases, judges order mediation and require parents to attempt to work out their own plan. Even in recommending counties, those where court-appointed counselors interview parents and send them on to either mediation, custody counseling, or probationary hearings, parents can ask for the opportunity to mediate. Many family-law systems automatically grant parents three sessions with the hope that mothers and fathers will create their own parenting schedules. Most mediation is confidential; generally, mediators do not make recommendations to the court or disclose what was said in sessions. When fears or hostility prevent parents from reaching agreements, the courts generally order them into custody counseling.

In custody counseling, couples are given a chance to create their own parenting schedule. If they are unable to cooperate, the counselor makes a recommendation to the judge. Typically judges follow counselors' recommendations and order parents to abide by them.

Fathers should initiate the mediation process. This demonstrates a willingness to reach a fair, expedient, and legal agreement, and at the same time allows Dad to take the lead in creating an agreement that is enforceable.

For example, if a recently divorced father has been the breadwinner of the family and now wants to co-parent, mediation is the place to start the process. His parenting agreement can include an outline of his plan to work progressively less and parent more. Men who say, "I'm not paying child support. I'm going to stay home with the kids like she does," won't be taken seriously if the children need the money he earns. The father must ease into working less as his ex-wife strives to work more. Often breadwinners need to allow at least two years for mothers to make the transition from homemaker to self-supporting parent. More and more mothers who want to hold fathers financially responsible indefinitely are being told by judges to get a job.

Jerry W., for example, was struggling financially two years after his divorce. He was caring for his children the majority of the time and paying child support to his ex-wife. His children's mother worked part-time as a waitress, four hours a day, two days a week, until the judge said, "I'll give you one week to find a job that pays enough for you to support yourself." Within a week, she was working full-time. Eventually, Jerry and his ex settled into working part-time jobs and co-parenting their children for equal lengths of time. For the past ten years, they have managed to work together to raise their children.

Working with Mediators

In most states, couples seeking a divorce will be sent into mediation. Many fathers are intimidated by court-ordered mediators and show up unprepared and feeling defensive. However, those who strive to benefit from the experience will listen closely to what the mediator has to say.

A wise father prepares himself in advance by speaking with other men who have been through the process and asking what they did to prepare themselves. Thus prepared, the father will feel confident in his plan and be better able to follow up on suggestions.

Since mediators see numerous cases, if prompted, they may suggest improvements to parenting plans. At the same time, fathers should be on the lookout for agreements that are unenforceable. It is up to the parents to make sure that what they agree upon is practical, maintainable, and legally binding.

A man we'll call Fred signed a co-parenting agreement with his ex-wife, Sheila, in court-ordered mediation. She was not happy with the arrangement but kept her concerns to herself. Sheila and Fred were to parent equally—one week on and one week off. Fred thought all the details were covered. The judge approved their plan, and it was recorded. The next week, however, Sheila refused to abide by their agreement and denied Fred access to their children.

One year later, when the two stood before the judge, she complained, "It feels as if he's trying to control my life."

Having not seen his children for fourteen months, Fred asked for a contempt of court order against Sheila for refusing him access to his kids. He was denied because the mother's attorney pointed out that a clause in the co-parenting agreement stating that the children would continue to practice the Jewish faith was unconstitutional. Fred was Jewish and the mother was not. Therefore, the ex-wife was not bound by the agreement. Legally, it was not her responsibility to maintain the children's faith. With a red face, the judge conceded and suggested to the father that he return to mediation. All the judge could do was to remind both parents that their children were being harmed by their inability to cooperate.

A father needs to anticipate what his ex-wife might say or do and prepare to respond accordingly. After all, no one knows an ex-wife like a former husband. Those who are prepared stand the best chance of reaching an agreement in mediation and of getting a positive recommendation from the custody counselor.

TWELVE TECHNIQUES TO ENHANCE MEDIATION

- Situate yourself so you won't be distracted by activities going on outside the mediation room. If there is a window, place your back to it.
- Arrive for mediation ten minutes early. One father showed up on time and found his ex-spouse socializing with their assigned mediator as if the two were sorority sisters.
- Show up with an understanding of parenting options and have your preferences well researched. Hard copy is best—for example, a visitation schedule marked on a calendar makes it easier for everyone to understand the father's plans.
- Bring a complete record—including canceled checks—of all child-support payments.
- When speaking or defending your position, be clear, logical, and assertive—but not aggressive.
- If your ex sounds blaming ("He's not capable of caring for the kids . . ."), ask, "What exactly do you need from me to be able to co-parent?" You might also remind her that blaming

undermines the opportunity to mediate. If necessary, ask the mediator to intercede.

- First impressions *are* important. When meeting with those who work in family law, show up well dressed. Present yourself as friendly and professional.

- Stay focused on your child's needs.

- Don't talk about what the ex-wife did in the past. If you appear bitter or vindictive, you will be perceived as a parent who is unwilling to cooperate.

- If your ex slanders you, in one sentence remind your past spouse of the most damaging thing she ever did to your children (use only as a means of establishing your boundaries and to motivate the mediator to take control of the session). Then immediately ask the mediator to "take control of the session." The point you want to make to your ex-wife is that you will cooperate, but you will not be a doormat.

- Be prepared with other options. What is the least you will accept? What might you bargain with or trade away?

- If you can get agreement on 70 percent of what you want, take it. You can work on the remaining 30 percent later.

More on Mediation and the Parenting Agreement

Clarke Dixon-Moses, a family mediator, shared the following observations:

"Even in the most successful mediations, both parties often feel that they have given up more than they wanted . . . And the fathers that seem to do well in family mediations are those who show up with a daily parenting plan, a weekly plan and a outline for the year. When you see someone who is that prepared it's hard not to take them seriously. Mediation spares parents a time-consuming court battle waged by attorneys charging hundreds of dollars an hour, and kids are spared the hostile environment created by warring parents."

Courts that require mediation often hear complaints from parents of bias by court-appointed mediators. If a mediator appears biased toward the mother, a father can respectfully ask for another mediator, preferably one who has lived the co-parenting experience. Occasionally the courts allow parents to change mediators. It is important, also, to remember that no matter how the mediation comes out, meditation itself is never the end of the process.

Mediation is a resource that can be used at any time. There are mediators who have private practices. Their rates are usually less than attorneys and, unlike an attorney, a mediator can empower both clients by encouraging them to seek what they want, understand all details, and look to the future.

When negotiating, prepare yourself emotionally, enter with confidence, use communication skills, don't be influenced by emotional displays, and continue to insist on your right to parent your children. As a committed parent, you can carry yourself with pride because, after all, you are a dedicated father, someone your children can be proud to emulate.

BE SURE THE PARENTING AGREEMENT MAKES CLEAR:
- Where the children will go to school
- What happens on holidays
- How the children will be exchanged (who drops them off, when, and where)
- That the child cannot be moved out of the county, even temporarily, without the court's approval and the other parent's knowledge and consent

Stick to the Agreement

Don't waver from the agreement unless absolutely necessary. Changing the parenting plan opens the door for confusion, misunderstanding, and resentment between mothers and fathers. For the protection of both parents, changes should be recorded with the courts immediately. Without a written record, agreements are forgotten, abandoned, and manipulated, and they become unenforceable.

For example, here is a situation that arises often: The parents have been bickering. Friday afternoon the father drives to his ex-wife's house to pick up his children for the weekend. His former spouse tells him that she is changing the visitation. She is going to take the kids to the park in the morning. He can pick up his kids tomorrow evening. The father is angry. He calls the police and reports his ex-spouse for denying him his children. The police ask, "What is the visitation schedule that appears on your court order?" The father remembers that the order, which has never been updated, allowed him to see his children four hours per night on Saturdays and Tuesdays only. He informs the police sergeant, who then says, "There is nothing I can do without a court order, and there is nothing you can do until court opens on Monday."

After a co-parenting schedule is recorded, continue to keep records of all financial transactions with your ex-spouse. Paying by check ensures you have a written record.

Changes should be researched and discussed with a counselor or knowledgeable friend before being presented to the ex-spouse for input. With good communication and mediation, parents can continue to minimize the impact of divorce on their children.

Consistency in the parenting schedule prevents children from feeling as if they are merely baggage being shuffled around at their parents' convenience.

If Mom and Dad have reached a mutually beneficial custody agreement without litigation, they each deserve the other's respect. As parents, they have demonstrated maturity, insight, and compassion by protecting their children from needless conflict.

Index

Communication
  with children, 7–8, 34–35,
    147–63, 181–83
  between parents, 106, 166–68,
    172, 179–84, 198–99,
    225–27
Consistency, 21–26, 122, 128,
  130–31, 142, 227
Co-parenting. *See also* Parenting
  benefits of, 129–31, 165–85
  problems with, 42–46, 165–76
  success with, 72–73, 80–82,
    177–82
Cotter, Holland, 133
Counseling, 79–80, 89, 106,
  220–21
Credit cards, 51–52

D
"Dad Door," 94
Daily care, 103–4
Dates, remembering, 26, 95–96
Dating
  boundaries for, 196–97
  considerations about, 187–200
  of ex-wife, 197–200
  opportunities for, 189–91
  tips for, 192–94
Deployment, 27–28, 30, 49–56,
  88–89. *See also* Military dads
Deployment forms, 209–19
Depression, 96, 98–100
Discipline, 8, 126–28, 146
Divorce
  coping with, 3, 9
  and court, 152–56, 168–71,
    220–27
  and dating, 187–200
  and mediation, 169–70, 183,
    220–27

preparing for, 38–48
statistics on, 43, 123–24
support for, 46, 48, 86–88,
  175, 178, 205
tips for, 17–21, 28–29
Divorced Fathers Network, 46,
  48, 86–88, 175, 178, 205
Divorce settlement, 152–56
Dixon-Moses, Clarke, 224
*Do What You Love, the Money
  Will Follow*, 84

E
Electronic communication, 7–8,
  48, 147–53, 181–82
"Electronic Communication,"
  152
Elementary-aged children, 20,
  105–20
E-mail, 7–8, 48, 147–50, 153,
  181–82
Emergencies, 51, 54–55, 96
Emergency plan, 97, 103
Emotions, showing, 107–10, 122
Empty nest, 141–42

F
Family and work, 10–11, 57–75
Family Care Plan, 54–55
Family law, 168–71, 220–27
Family meetings, 19–20
Farrell, Warren, 24, 92
Father, success as, 72–73, 80–82,
  177–82, 201–2
Father and Child Reunion, 92
Father figures, 4–5
Fatherless homes, 5–6, 123–24,
  133
Fatherly love, 201–2